Hunter Diack was born in Aberdeenshire in 1908 and was educated at the Universities of Aberdeen and Toronto. Until 1974 he was senior lecturer in education at the University of Nottingham. He was a radio critic for the *Times Literary Supplement* and theatre critic for the *Spectator*. His researches into language and vocabulary led him to make many television and radio broadcasts, and to publish a number of educational books. Hunter Diack wrote two autobiographical books, BOY IN A VILLAGE and THAT VILLAGE ON THE DON. His STANDARD READING TESTS was written in conjunction with J. C. Daniels.

Hunter Diack

Wordpower

Your Vocabulary and its Measurement

Paladin

Granada Publishing Limited
First published in Great Britain in 1975 by Paladin
Frogmore, St Albans, Herts AL2 2NF

Standard Literacy Tests first published in Great Britain by
Hart-Davis Educational Ltd 1975
Copyright © Estate of Hunter Diack 1975
Made and printed in Great Britain by
Cox and Wyman Ltd, London, Reading and Fakenham
Set in Monotype Ehrhardt

Introduction

How many words do you know? The tests in this book will give you an answer. There are 50 tests and each word you know in any one of them stands for 600 words in your total *general* vocabulary. If, for example, you know 30 words in one of the tests, your total general vocabulary will be 30 × 600 words approximately, i.e. 18,000. There are only 60 words in each of the tests and you may find it difficult to believe that so small a sample can give you even a rough measurement of vocabularies that may run into tens of thousands of words.

By the time you have read this introduction, however, you will no longer find it surprising. The description given later of how the tests were constructed will show you that it is all a matter of applying common sense. In any case, we do not rely on one test of sixty words but, as a precaution, take the average score in three tests.

A fair proportion of those who have measured their vocabularies by the tests have commented on the remarkable consistency of the scores in the three tests. In about one case out of fifty, however, an odd concatenation of probabilities produces a set of scores in which the highest differs from the lowest by what seems an unreasonable amount. In many instances I have been able to give an additional test and every time I have done so the fourth score was close to the two scores that differed least from one another. So if, by some freak of chance, when you do three tests, you find your scores are of this order: 44, 35, 38, and you then do a fourth test there is a very high probability that your fourth score will be between 34 and 39.

Using the Tests

The bulk of this introduction is concerned with various aspects of the background and the implications of the tests, but no doubt at this stage readers will be more interested in how to measure vocabulary according to a stricter procedure than is suggested by the very general statements I have made so far. So next I describe the procedure that was followed under research conditions. The most concise way of describing the procedure is to give the relevant part of the form that students who were being formally tested were asked to fill in:

Literacy Test

Read through the words in the test in the order as numbered. When you come to a word to which you cannot give at least one acceptable meaning, enter the *number* of that word in the first of the ten squares printed below. Then carry on reading through the test until you come to the next word you are not sure of. Enter the number of that word in the next square. Carry on in the same way until you have filled all the squares with a number. At that point stop reading through the test. Now, in the five numbered spaces, show in writing that you really do know at least one acceptable meaning for each of the five last words you claimed to know, i.e. the last five words whose numbers you did not enter in the squares. You can show your knowledge of the word by giving a synonymous term or phrase, by using it in a sentence that demonstrates your knowledge, or you can do it by diagram or sketch.

<table>
<tr><td> </td><td> </td><td> </td><td> </td><td> </td><td> </td><td> </td><td> </td><td> </td><td> </td></tr>
</table>

1. ....

....

2. ....

....

3. ....

....

4. ....

....

5. ....

....

You don't need to draw up a form like that in order to measure your own vocabulary, but if you are to get as accurate a measure as the tests can give you, you will have to follow in essence the instructions given on the form.

Having produced written evidence of your knowledge of the last five words you claimed to know, you must then check the correctness of your answers with a dictionary. If all five answers are right, then you are entitled to assume that all your previous unwritten answers were also correct. Your score in the test is the number of words you had right. Follow the same procedure with two more of the tests. That will give you three test marks. Take the average of these. Multiply that average by 600 and that is your total vocabulary. Here is an example:

$$\begin{array}{ll} \text{Score 1} & 36 \\ \text{Score 2} & 38 \\ \text{Score 3} & 34 \\ \text{Total} & 108 \end{array} \qquad \text{Average } \frac{108}{3} = 36$$

$$\text{Total vocabulary } 36 \times 600 = 21{,}600$$

If your thinking is so straight that your five written answers are all right, there is a very simple way of finding how many words you knew in a test. Just subtract ten from the last of the ten numbers you wrote down. That's obvious if you *suddenly* come to an end of the words you knew and all the ten numbers are then in sequence, but your word-knowledge does not always cut off with a sharp edge like that. You may find yourself with a string of numbers like this –

$$29 \quad 33 \quad 36 \quad 39 \quad 40 \quad 41 \quad 42 \quad 43 \quad 44 \quad 45$$

– such a list is quite typical. It still remains true, however, that the total of words known in that test is the last number of the list less ten, i.e. thirty-five.

Suppose, however, things turn out at the opposite extreme and that all your five written answers are wrong. What then? The first thing to do in a case like that is to sit back for as long as it takes to let the idea sink into your mind that you may have been going through life with the most vague idea of the meanings of many of the words you have encountered in your reading – or indeed in conversation. The other interpretation is even less comfortable; it is that you are too determined to have a good opinion of yourself in the matter of wordpower. You go so far as to deceive yourself into thinking that you know for certain what you are only guessing at.

There are two ways of dealing with this situation in the narrow field of vocabulary measurement. One is to go back through the test, dictionary at hand, checking your idea of the meaning of each word until you come to those you cannot possibly have any doubt about – this will give you a more realistic measure. The other way is to begin all over again with another test and be stricter with yourself this time.

Those same procedures should be adopted if three or four of your written answers are wrong, but if one or two only are wrong you need only subtract the appropriate number – one or two – from your score for that test.

Interpreting Your Score

Now that you have measured your vocabulary, you will be interested to know how your vocabulary-rating places you in relation to other people, and what is implied by a vocabulary-rating at all.

The number of words in your general vocabulary is an indication of the width and quality of your reading. If your vocabulary is significantly higher than that of your dearest enemy, then you can claim that you have read more widely than he has – that's the width. You can also comfort yourself with the knowledge that if you and he were to read the same book you would read it with a richer understanding than he would – that's the quality. There is, however, a qualification to be made to this latter statement. This other fellow may be a narrow specialist in some line – electronics, photography, collecting butterflies – your larger general vocabulary will not put you on the same level in reading books on his special subject.

The word 'significantly' used just now may still be hanging around, an unanswered question, in the antechambers of your mind. 'Significantly higher'? How high is that? The various investigations of which glimpses appear later in this introduction point to a difference of not less than 2,400 words as being a significant difference in terms of total general vocabulary. The reason for making it 2,400 and not the round figure of 2,000 is that the tests go in multiples of 600 and a difference of 4 points in the average of three test scores is the minimum that I would regard as significant – that differential is equal to a difference of 2,400 words.

Fortunately, it is possible to be more precise about the implications of different sizes of vocabulary.

The different levels in the tests stand for the following levels of vocabulary:

Level 1 – 6,000 words
Level 2 – 12,000 words
Level 3 – 18,000 words
Level 4 – 24,000 words
Level 5 – 30,000 words
Level 6 – 36,000 + words

If you are more than twenty years old, your score on these tests will have been over 25 – probably between 30 and 40, may even have been as high as 50 – but is as unlikely to have been over 55 as it is to have been under 25.

Statements like these can be made with a high degree of confidence because of the dependability of the test scores and because of a certain consistency of relationship between scores, age of the scorers and some types of behaviour.

For example, a lack of the intellectual curiosity that would lead to the reading of this book is bound to be one of the characteristics of anyone who has grown up in an English-speaking community like ours and has reached the age of twenty without acquiring a vocabulary of more than 15,000 words – the level indicated by a score of 25. You have the intellectual curiosity to read this book. Therefore if you are 20 years old or more, you will have scored more than 25.

The number 15,000 in this context may be thought surprising by many people because one of the most widely believed myths about language is that we need no more than a few hundred different words in order to carry on the ordinary business of life. That myth originated with the work of C. K. Ogden who in his 'Basic English' reduced the essential vocabulary of English to 800 words and claimed very persuasively that everything that needed to be said could be said by means of those 800 words with the addition of some technical terms. So persuasive was he in this and in his propaganda in favour of Basic English as an international language that the government during Churchill's premiership voted a substantial sum of public money to further the cause of Basic English as an international language. The only traceable result of those good intentions has been the furtherance of the myth that people use and need far fewer words than they actually do. When you think of the names of birds, trees, flowers, parts of cars and all the fairly special terms necessary for carrying on the ordinary business of life in such a complicated society as this, the myth explodes itself.

The adult with a vocabulary of no more than 15,000 words has neither intellectual curiosity nor mental enterprise. Nearly all those with the kind of interest that would lead them to read *Wordpower* will have vocabularies of 18,000 or more. On the other hand only about 25 per cent of them will score over 40 in the tests, i.e. will have vocabularies of 24,000 words or over. A few will score 50 or over, but so far I have not seen anyone scoring more than 55.

These were the things I had in mind when I wrote that your score probably lay between 30 and 40.

You may have noticed that I made no distinction between men and women in estimating vocabularies. That is because I have not found one among adults. It has for years been quite well established that infant girls are quicker to learn to speak than boys but that difference is not maintained for more than a year or two and thereafter the growth of vocabulary for both sexes is a matter of environment and individual learning-power. Generally speaking, vocabularies go on developing by several hundred words a year – over a thousand among the quicker learners – for as long as formal education goes on – whether that formal education is full-time or part-time.

A picture of the development of vocabularies and some interesting glimpses of the sociology of language is to be had by examining 'population' of each of the vocabulary levels.

Level 1   0–6,000 words

Most of those who score between 0–10 are children between the ages of 6 and 9. Older backward children are in this group and so also are all adult illiterates. These adults fall into this group not because they have a speaking vocabulary of under 6,000 – though some may be intellectually under-developed to that extent – but, ironically, because they cannot begin to do the tests in the manner intended, since they cannot read.

Level 2   6,000–12,000 words

If your score in the tests was 40 or over, then it is quite likely that when you were a child of ten you were near the top of the Level 2 group, with a vocabulary of 12,000 words. Probably about a quarter of the adult population of the country have vocabularies no greater than 12,000.

Level 3   12,000–18,000 words

Counting adults only, this is the most populous of the 6 Levels. In the lower half of it, in the range 12,000–15,000, are most of those adults who left school as soon as the law would allow them and have done hardly any reading since. In the range 15,000–18,000 are to be found also adults who left school as soon as they could but who for some reason or other found it necessary to continue with some reading or who were in jobs that involved language study of one kind or another – as, for example, secretarial work.

One would expect eighteen-year-olds in full-time education and intending to go on to further education to have reached the top of this range.

Level 4   18,000–24,000 words

In this range we find mature adults who though they may not have had more than the legal minimum of full-time education have nevertheless lively minds and have maintained a keen interest in what is going on in the world. Vocabularies in this range indicate a fairly wide range of reading. The majority of university undergraduates have vocabularies in this range – so also do members of most of the professions with some years' experience.

Level 5   24,000–30,000 words

Men and women in this range are among the most widely read in the country. They are to be found in the top echelons of their professions or heading in that direction.

Level 6   30,000–36,000 words

Those few who fall into this category are the same as those in the previous category only more so. With Level 5, however, we have, one might say, reached the end of the serious purposes of the tests. At Level 6 they become more an intellectual game than a means of scientific measurement.

That, then, is the general picture of the test Levels in relation to the adult population of the country. Statistically, there is a definite relationship between size of vocabulary and the amount of responsibility attached to the job occupied. It does not follow, however, that the possession of an extensive vocabulary is a guarantee of a responsible job; it may be better regarded as a guarantee of wide reading and wide contacts with life and these in turn may lead to the job of high responsibility.

When a small set of these literacy tests was published early in 1973, I had many letters about them. There was one from an ex-coal-miner who wondered about the reliability of the tests because it showed him to have the vocabulary of a university graduate. The letter was written in a style that suggested he had as good a knowledge of the English language as many a university graduate – and better than some. There was another from a local government employee who wrote to say he thought I'd be interested to know that though he was the only one in his office without a university degree he yet had the highest score of them all. I heard, too, from an office clerk who scored significantly higher than the office-manager. But one gets a very one-sided picture from correspondence. A bank-manager would never write to say he thought I'd be interested to know that he scored less in the tests than one of the girls on the counter. I did find one university undergraduate, however, whose knowledge of words began to falter at Level 2.

Counting Words

In the autumn of 1973 it was announced that a computer team at some American university was to produce a more extensive survey than had so far been done of word-frequencies in current English. The purpose of the project was not stated and I cannot think of any satisfactory one. About fifty years ago a major educational psychologist of the day, Thorndike, got a team together to count and record all the words that appeared in general reading matter, together with an indication of their frequency of occurrence. The reason he gave for initiating this enterprise was that a list of the kind proposed would be very useful to the writers, editors and publishers of educational material. The assumption behind it all was that there was a direct relationship between a word's frequency of occurrence in print and the age of the readers it was suitable for. This business of counting the frequency of occurrence of words went on – with some interruptions no doubt – for about twenty-five years. There were various reports and publications during that time, but the final outcome was the publication of an alphabetical list of 30,000 words each with a set of figures opposite it showing how often it had appeared in various types of reading matter. Altogether 18,000,000 words of running text were analysed in this way. I found the final Thorndike list of some slight use in compiling the Literacy Tests – but I doubt if it was ever of any real use to the writers of educational books as a help in fitting vocabulary to age. In fact some curious books would have been produced if the word-frequency list had been taken as a precise guide. For example, no one would have encountered the word *carrot* in print before the age of fourteen, and the word *parsnip* would not have been encountered in reading-matter graded on this frequency scale until the student had reached mature years and was possibly engaged in research work – perhaps into some aspect of word-frequency. *Parsnip* had some odd bed-fellows. These are a few of the words that also landed in the category of once-in-a-million words of running text: *acrobat, adrift, affidavit, announcer, aphorism, apostate, appendicitis, confectioner* ... Any child understands the word *acrobat*, but there's many an adult who would have to rack his brains to produce a valid definition of *aphorism*. It is obvious, then, that you cannot devise an accurate measure of vocabulary by simply going to a word-frequency list and picking out words according to their frequency-rating to produce a list in which the first word is of high frequency, the last of low frequency and the others are ranged in steps in between.

How then did one produce a measure of vocabulary? The orthodox way was to take a sample of words from a dictionary and if your sample was a valid one, then you would know the same proportion of the total words in the dictionary as you did of the sample. The reason for working from a sample, of course, was sheer economy of time. A substantial dictionary like *Webster's Third International* has about 450,000 entries. It would take a fair number of evenings for a man to go through that lot ticking off the words he knew and keeping a tally of them. There are, however, different ways of extracting a sample from a dictionary. One of the commonest was to extract a word at regular points throughout the dictionary. You might, for example, take the first word on every tenth page throughout the dictionary. With the *Concise Oxford* that would give you about one hundred and fifty words. If you knew a hundred of these, you might think you are entitled to claim that you know two-thirds of the words in that dictionary. But you'd be wrong. That method of sampling cannot possibly produce a valid sample because it is usually the commonest words that take up most space in a dictionary. The word *as*, for example, takes up more than a column in the *Concise Oxford* while the word *apostate* takes only three lines. If you imagine all the words in the dictionary, with their definitions, derivations, etc., stretched out in a line, each entry taking up as much space as in the dictionary itself, and if you further imagine that you are to pick out a word at approximately ten foot intervals, counting the two columns per page as approximately one foot in length, then you will have no difficulty in realizing how heavily weighted this method is towards giving you a sample in which the commoner words predominate. Faulty sampling of that kind was one of the reasons for the huge vocabularies research workers in America discovered among quite ordinary people. Six-year-old children, for example, were found to have an average vocabulary of 23,000 words – ranging from 6,000 to 48,000; eighteen-year-olds were found to have an average vocabulary of 80,300, ranging from 30,700 to 136,500 and every member of a group of college graduates was found to have a vocabulary of more than 200,000 words. These are fairy-tale figures even though they are to be found in classic psychological text-books. My reason for flatly denying the reliability of figures is that among a considerable number of men and women accomplished in the use of English and mature in their professions I have not found one who was familiar with all of the words in a 40,000-word dictionary. There's another reason besides poor sampling that leads to such gross exaggerations, the habit some of the word-counters had of counting derived words as words in their own right, e.g. *boy*, *boys*, *boy's*, *boyish*, *boyishness*, and *boyhood* count as seven words in one American list. You can soon bump up a vocabulary by that kind of arithmetic.

Each of the literacy tests in this book is of course a sixty-word sample from the total vocabulary of English and the reader who has had the limits of his vocabulary delineated by means of these samples has a right to know, and probably will be interested in knowing, how these samples were arrived at. The idea came to me in two parts: 1 Everyone acquires his vocabulary in a particular order, one word after the other. 2 Though the order is different from one person to the next, there is a considerable amount of overlap, e.g. everyone brought up in an English-speaking community learns the word *breakfast* before he learns the word *seriation*.

Before this flash of the obvious brought its thunder to my mind, I had already been working for some months classifying words according to a system that took into account level of difficulty and frequency of occurrence – in speech as well as in print. I had often checked the allocations to the various classes by trying out samples in tests given to school pupils, students in various kinds of establishments, college and university staffs, and indeed anyone who would co-operate. As soon as I realized the importance of the order in which words were likely to be learned, I came by a much clearer picture of what my job was. I was constructing a set of probes to be inserted at different *levels* of vocabulary development. It may seem an artificially tidy arrangement to have six Levels, with each word at each Level standing for 600 words of general vocabulary, and further, to have 6,000 words at each Level. But in fact that is the way it worked out. I was not conscious of imposing that pattern on the language. It was more as if that symmetry was there waiting to be revealed. I had indeed set out with a rather different notion, with the idea of trying to classify the vocabulary of English into ten categories. That was something I did not find possible. Going on the basis, as I originally did, of 'difficulty' and 'frequency of occurrence', I could not find more than six categories into which I could fit the words. Nor was it possible when I switched to 'time-order' as the basis of classification.

Matters of Chance

The measurement of vocabulary is, of course, a statistical operation and perhaps highly sophisticated statistical techniques could have been brought into play in constructing these tests. I did not find it necessary to go further than simple arithmetic and I have a feeling that if sophisticated statistical techniques could have done this job, it would have already been done, for, now that the hard drudgery has been taken out of statistics by electronic devices, every year brings a new army of potential research workers hungry for statistical problems against which to pit their electronically-assisted wits.

The first 6,000 words that two people acquire will not be the same words – the difference will not only be in the order but in the actual words as well. In the case of twins there will be less difference than between two people brought up in different environments, but the vocabularies of even identical twins will not be identical. So if you listed all the words in any two 6,000-word vocabularies, you would find more than 6,000 different words. How many more? Anything from 'several' to 'a lot more than you'd expect'. But, quite certainly, if you could bring together a million 6,000-word vocabularies, you would certainly be far, far short of having a million different words in them – there are not that many words in the English language. How far short of a million? I estimate that if you took all the 6,000-word vocabularies in one of the major English-speaking societies – the British or the North American, for example – and listed all the standard English words in them, the total of different words would not exceed 12,000 by very much. I am able to be more precise on this point than I was when only two vocabularies were involved because of the nature of language.

When a vocabulary as small as 6,000 words is being considered, the minds being considered are immature – whatever the age of the bodies in which they are 'housed'. Minds with a 6,000-word limitation on them are incapable of taking part in the kind of thinking we commonly call 'abstract' – and 12,000 is about the limit of words in the language that can occur in contexts where only the lowest levels of abstraction are involved. The variations between one society and another will be due either to usage, e.g. *side-walk* instead of *pavement* or facets of the external environment, e.g. different trees, different ways of cooking and different names for cooked dishes. In vocabularies so limited, however, these differences will not be great. I should think in fact that 12,500 would cover all the Standard English words that appear in 6,000-word vocabularies anywhere or indeed have at any time appeared in vocabularies so limited – and there was a time when even your vocabulary was of that calibre. If, in spite of the millions of 6,000-word vocabularies that existed or now exist, only about 12,000 different words have been involved, then there must be a very great amount of overlap between vocabularies. After all, thousands of millions of vocabularies have passed through that phase of development and you may think that the phenomenon of two 6,000-word vocabularies having the same words in common and those words having been acquired in the same order must be of quite frequent occurrence. However, strange though it may seem at first glance, the odds are against that occurring; for the number of different combinations of 6,000 words that can be got out of 12,000 is very great indeed. A mathematical physicist I talked to about this said it reminded him of the number of atoms that early this century had been calculated to exist in the universe. There must, of course, be a considerable amount of sheer speculation in an attempt to calculate the number of atoms in the universe or even in your little finger, but the number of 6,000-word combinations that can be got from 12,000 words is precisely calculable. It is a

matter of 'long multiplication'. Very long multiplication. You begin by multiplying 12,000 by 11,999. Having got an answer to that, you then multiply that answer by 11,998. You multiply that answer by 11,997 . . . and so you carry on multiplying by one less each time until you come to 6,001 which is your last multiplier. There is no need for you to work through the whole operation to realize that the result is a number of great magnitude. It broke the bank in the only computer one of my mathematical friends had available when I asked him if he'd work it out for me by that means. So I can give only an approximation to a number you now know how to work out precisely for yourself. The number, then, if written out in full without any mathematical shorthand, would be *considerably* greater than 12,000,
000,000,000,000,000,000,000,000,000,000,000,000,000,000,000,
000,000,000,000,000,000,000,000,000,000,000,000,000,000,000,
000,000,000,000,000,000,000,000,000,000,000,000,000,000.000,
000,000,000,000,000,000,000,000,000,000,000,000,000,000,000,
. . . and so on for the next eighteen pages.

Yet only 12,000 different words are involved in that colossal number of different combinations.

Although, theoretically, my aim was to select for each test at Level 1 a set of words likely to appear in the 6,000th place in a vocabulary, the chances against success were not as great as they may seem. There were in fact about 2,600 words likely to occupy that position. Furthermore even if one of the words I chose occupied the 4,001st position in a particular vocabulary, it would still carry the implication that that was a vocabulary of 6,000 words because in 85 per cent of vocabularies its presence signified the presence of another 1,599 of that group of words in the positions between the 4,000th and 6,000th place. There were in fact 2,000 'right answers'. If I selected the right 2,600 words, any ten of them would do at this Level in a test.

I have given these glimpses of the statistical background to show that the tests are far from being hit-or-miss affairs. It was for the low-level vocabularies that most detailed information of a statistical kind was available but similar principles obtained through the next four Levels.

The stipulation that you must find ten words you don't know before you stop is of course a simple statistical device that increases the chance of accuracy in the final measure. It takes into account the fact that the Levels cannot be separated with complete rigidity. By sheer accident a single word at Level 3 may have been unknown to you – but you still have a chance of making up by knowing one of the words at Level 4 or even going on to Level 5. On the other hand, if you are a genuine Level 4 person, you will gain no credit for the lucky chance of knowing one of the Level 6 words for your allotted ten 'not known' spaces will be all used up by then.

One question of a simple statistical nature was put to me that I think I should answer here. It was: 'Your Level 1 words are, you say, typical of 6,000-word vocabularies, your Level 2 words typical of 12,000-word vocabularies – and so on. Since you go up in steps of 6,000 words, how can you claim to measure vocabularies in between?'

The answer is best given by a specific example. A man scored 35 in the test. He knew all the words to the end of Level 3, i.e. up to No. 30. He then knew Nos. 32, 33, 35, 36, 37. There was therefore no doubt according to the test that he had a vocabulary of over 18,000. On the other hand he had not produced the ten pieces of evidence the test would have allowed him to claim that he had a vocabulary of 24,000. He knew five words at the 24,000 level but there were five words at that level that he did not know. The interpretation therefore is that he may have a vocabulary of 24,000 words, but we can't say for certain, and the evidence suggests that we can with much more certainty say that his vocabulary is half-way between 18,000 and 24,000. In that particular case the evidence from the other two tests, in which he scored 34 and 35, supported that conclusion.

I felt that by that time I had acquired what I had come to think of as 'the feel of the dictionary' – and since dictionaries played such a big part in the construction of the tests, it is perhaps appropriate for me now to give some account of the trials and tribulations that came to me through dictionaries – and of course the help these indispensable volumes gave me.

Dictionaries

Dictionaries are popularly believed to be full of meanings. 'You don't know the meaning of that word? Well, you know where to find it, don't you? The dictionary.' What literate person has not at some time been told that? What literate person has not handed on that valuable piece of misinformation to someone less literate than himself? For, of course, it is a piece of misinformation. There are no meanings in any dictionary; there never were. There is in any dictionary, cheap or expensive, compact or extensive, nothing but printed signs that stand for words. When, following the advice so freely distributed, you look up a word in a dictionary, you don't find a meaning printed alongside it, you find a string of words and/or phrases and the bigger the dictionary, the longer the string. If you and the dictionary are working well together, you will find among those equivalent, or near-equivalent words or phrases, one or two that will lead you down the path of recollected experience to the meaning you are seeking, for it is in your experience – perceptual, intellectual, emotional, spiritual – and there only, that your meanings lie.

Have you ever – using a compressed dictionary more useful for checking spellings than anything else – had this experience? You are looking for the meaning of a word. The pocket dictionary gives as its equivalent another word you don't know the meaning of. So you look up this second word. And what do you find? The very word that started you off on the inquiry – and there you're stranded, right back where you started from. This illustrates the fact that there is no meaning in a dictionary. Well-edited dictionaries never send you on such blatantly circular tours but the best edited dictionary cannot provide you with meanings directly. That this is so is more obvious at some times than at others.

Look up the word *symphony* in the *Concise Oxford* and, after the archaic usage for which 'harmony' is given as the equivalent, you read 'sonata for full orchestra'. But you may not have a meaning for the word *sonata*, so you turn to the appropriate page in the dictionary and for the word *sonata* you read 'composition for one instrument (e.g. piano) or two (e.g. piano and violin), normally with three or four movements (one or more being usually in sonata form) contrasted in rhythm and speed but related in key'. But what is 'sonata form'? That is dealt with in a sub-entry: 'type of composition in which two themes ('subjects') are successively set forth, developed and restated'.

These definitions are not meanings; they are the best the editors of the dictionary could do to provide a guide towards meanings for the words *symphony* and *sonata*, but the editors knew perfectly well that their attempts would mean nothing to anyone who had not had experience of listening to sonatas and symphonies.

The dictionaries I used in compiling the literacy tests were the *Concise Oxford*, *Everyman's English Dictionary*, and *Chambers's Twentieth Century*. To a lesser extent I used the *Oxford Illustrated* and I made occasional excursions to Roget's *Thesaurus* and to Thorndike and Lorge's frequency-tabulated collection of

30,000 words. Naturally I developed an interest in how the minds of dictionary-editors worked. So on occasion curiosity led me to consult the big *Oxford Dictionary*, *Webster's Third New International* and the *Random House Dictionary*.

One of the first things I discovered about dictionaries when I approached them from the how-many-words-do-you-know angle was that it is not at all easy to find out how many words a dictionary deals with, i.e. gives equivalents for. I thought that would be one of the easiest things to determine. In fact I thought I would not have to determine it. I expected it to be merely a matter of looking in the editorial preface and there I would find this valuable information. But in neither the *Concise Oxford* nor *Chambers's* was such information to be found. *Everyman's*, however, informed me that its coverage totalled 48,737 words and 6,618 phrases. The total of 48,737 words, however, included a considerable number of derived words that would not count as separate words for the purposes of the literacy tests. So even when the editorial preface did give the kind of information I was looking for, I could not accept it. Of course one could hardly expect the editor of a dictionary to claim that the volume contained fewer words than it did.

Various complications affected the selection of words for the tests.

The word *rat* as a verb meaning *desert* might well have been one of the Level 3 words, but I could not use it because of the commoner meaning of the word which is normally learned so early in life that it does not qualify for inclusion even at Level 1. Only by setting the words in specific contexts could I have included such words in their less common – and therefore later acquired – usages. That, however, would have defeated one of the purposes of the tests, which was to provide a measuring device that would bring an accurate result as quickly as possible.

At the beginning of this introduction I suggested that you might be surprised at the claim that by means of a mere sixty words vocabularies of many thousands of words could be measured with reasonable accuracy, but no doubt you will have noticed that in fact the number of words necessary is fewer even than that. Most adults can assume knowledge of the first twenty words in each of the tests and can with equal confidence assume ignorance of the last ten. Indeed, when I was testing mature students, if the time available was limited, I told them to begin at word number twenty-one on the assumption that they undoubtedly knew all the words at the first two Levels. So in those cases the operative words did not exceed thirty. Economy on that scale could not have been achieved had I decided to put the words in context. In any case the use of contexts in order to test knowledge of particular meanings of certain words would not have increased the accuracy of the measure at all. The fact that the tests do not call upon you to show that you know that *rat* may mean *desert* is of no consequence. A score of 30 in the tests indicates a vocabulary of approximately 18,000; there is a high probability that among those 18,000 words the word *rat* meaning *desert* occurs; with a score of 35 that probability turns into as near certainty as makes no difference.

In the *Concise Oxford* the word *cross* appears as two separate head-words. These are followed by *cross-* with a hyphen also as a head-word. Then come twenty-six head-words of which *cross-* is the first half. In the middle of that lot comes the head-word *crosse*. On the opposite page the words *croup*, *crow*, *crowd* and *crown* all appear as head-words more than once. In fact there are not many pages in the dictionary which do not have repetitions of that kind. I did not become seriously involved with the question as to whether *light* meaning the opposite of *dark* and *light* meaning the opposite of *heavy* were one or two words. As far as the measurement of vocabulary was concerned *light* was one word. This meant, of course, that the number of different head-words in the *Concise Oxford* was considerably less than the 36,000 my calculations indicated. However, the losses due to these repetitions are well compensated for by compound words that appear not as head-words but as sub-entries. For example, the word *crow*, referred to a few sentences back, appears thrice as a head-word, but as sub-entries there are *crowbar*, *crowbill*, *crowfoot*, *crow-quill*, *crow's nest* and *crow-toe*. Throughout the dictionary there were enough of these, I felt, to justify my estimate of 36,000 words as the measuring-rod for general vocabulary.

Any page opened at random in a dictionary of the kind I have been dealing with is likely to give you evidence of these complications.

I have just tested that statement opening the *Concise Oxford* at random. The first three head-words at the top of the left-hand column of the left-hand page are *full*[2], *fuller*[1] and *fuller*[2]. The definition given of *full*[2] is 'cleanse and thicken (cloth)'. *Fuller*[1] is defined as 'one who fulls cloth' and *fuller*[2] is given the lengthier definition: 'grooved tool on which iron is shaped; groove made by this, especially on horse-shoes; (vb. stamp with fuller)'. Because *full*[1], which is on the previous page, belongs to what might be called Level o on the test-scale, I could not have used any of these head-words in the tests. I could, however, have used *fuller's earth* which appears as a sub-entry to *fuller*[1]. That puts *fuller* into a context and so selects a particular meaning, but it does so without wasting words or time. The first time I ever heard of fuller's earth I was told it was some chemical substance and, on the analogy of Beecham's pills, put it to the credit of some chemist called Fuller. The word *earth* puzzled me at that time, for then I did not know of that definition of *earth* that goes: 'any of certain metallic oxides, uninflammable and having little taste or smell', a definition that would put that common word *earth* into the Level 5 category. There are a number of compounds in which *earth* appears that would enable that word to appear at various Levels. Not all those I give here are to be found in the *Concise Oxford*, so if you want to know the meaning of *earth-drake*, *earth-flax*, *earth-mad* or *earth-tongue*, for example, you will have to go to another dictionary. You won't find the meaning there, of course, but you will find some words that will lead you to those aspects of your experience in which the meanings of those words lie. Here is the list: *earth-apple*, *earth-board*, *earth-bound*, *earth-bred*, *earth-drake*, *earth-flax*, *earth-mad*, *earth-nut*, *earthquake*, *earth-shaking*, *earth-shine*, *earth-table*, *earth-tongue*, *earth-work* and *earthworm*.

Extending Your Vocabulary

One of the claims with which psychologists surprised the rest of the world a few decades ago was that they had proved that in human beings intelligence stops developing about the age of sixteen. That was a staggering claim to make but there seemed to be so much evidence to support it that it eventually became widely accepted and was incorporated into the mythology of psychological science. Nowadays psychologists are much more cautious about making statements involving the term 'intelligence' even though they have done little about exploding the myth about intelligence ceasing to grow in mid-adolescence. Yet in spite of vast statistical tables on the subject there never was a scrap of evidence in support of the claim. All that was proved was that it is possible to devise mental tests in which, on the average, sixteen-year-olds score as highly as adults.

It is very much to the point that no vocabulary test entitled to be called a test could ever be produced in which sixteen-year-olds would score as well as adults, for our vocabularies go on increasing for as long as we are mentally alive. The increase is not regular from year to year. Indeed normally there is a sharp fall in the rate of increase when contact with formal education comes to an end, for people will not add words to their vocabularies unless for some reason or other they feel a need to. Formal education plays a very large part here because that is so very much a matter of learning new words and how to manipulate them.

It may be taken as a socio-linguistic law that, in general, people acquire no bigger a vocabulary than they need to carry on the business of living in the environment that chance (and/or good or bad management) has placed them in. That is the simple fact behind the high correlation that is found between vocabulary-ratings and the kinds of job that people do. A lawyer needs a bigger vocabulary to qualify in his job than a lathe-operator does; there is a bigger vocabulary of law than of lathe-operating and the law-student's training is largely a matter of learning that vocabulary. When he is in practice the lawyer's day-to-day business is very much a matter of interpreting and using words. So he is never out of touch with language in a fairly elaborate form. The lathe-operator has indeed to learn the language of that particular branch of engineering but that is small compared with the vocabulary of law and in the practice of his job language plays a minimal role; he has, therefore, little stimulus from that source towards the acquisition of a large vocabulary.

One might think that in a job classed as 'secretary-typist' in the Situations Vacant columns there would be an environment favourable to vocabulary development, but that does not necessarily follow. The variety of jobs that appear under that heading is too great to allow that generalization to be made. Some secretary-typists spend their time addressing envelopes and typing letters that are purely routine in style and content. On the other hand there are secretary-typists with jobs that bring them in contact with heads of business empires or top-level administrators in local authorities or in government departments. Such jobs are likely to make much greater demands.

The wide variety of types of work done under a single heading like 'secretary-typist' might affect the results of a formal investigation into the correlation between type of job and extent of vocabulary, but any investigation that did not show a high correlation would have some weakness like not distinguishing accurately enough between the different types of work done by people who are listed as having the same occupation. The correlation is, of course, not perfect, because people's environments are not wholly determined by their jobs. Trade union contacts may lead a man or woman in a fairly routine job to acquire an extensive political vocabulary; a dramatized version of a novel on television may lead to further reading and the acquisition of a bigger vocabulary.

What can be guaranteed, however, is that, family influence and similar things apart, no one will get or hold down a job for which he does not have the vocabulary. That's another sociolinguistic law. So there are good practical reasons for trying to increase your vocabulary.

On what may reasonably be regarded as a higher level there lies the further truth that the richer your vocabulary is the richer your mind is likely to be. An increase of vocabulary is likely also to affect your personality – in ways, however, too various for me to generalize about, though I would like to express the hope that no strong silent man will as a result of following the advice I am about to give turn into a pompously speaking ass.

There are some people who think that if a person sets out to increase his vocabulary he is faking things. A certain hankering after my old philosophy keeps me sympathetic towards that point of view, but does not prevent me from thinking that anybody who does not take the trouble to get as near as possible to the meaning of the words he reads is either lazy or stupid, and if in addition he pretends to understand what he has read, then he is as guilty of faking as anybody who sets out to acquire a larger vocabulary as part of the process of more fully understanding what he hears or reads.

A good English dictionary is the only source you can depend on for increasing your knowledge of the vocabulary of the English language and the way you use a dictionary will depend on your attitude towards it. Some people speak of 'the dictionary' as though it were a volume of biblical authority. They take it down from the shelf only on rare occasions as the final arbiter in settling arguments about meaning or spelling. That isn't making the best use of it; it's setting a dictionary too far apart from the ordinary business of using the language.

There's another curious attitude towards English dictionaries that one finds noticeably among English students. They do not quite resent the existence of English-for-the-English dictionaries, but they do seem to resent having to consult one. It's as though they felt it a blow to their self-esteem to have to consult a dictionary in order to understand sentences written in their own language. If they are studying, say, French, they automatically assume that a French-English, English-French dictionary is the main tool for the job. But rather than admit to themselves that they don't really know the meaning of an English word, they'll guess at it from the context and may go on for years with off-track ideas of what certain words mean. That also is an unprofitable attitude to take towards a dictionary of English.

Unfortunately pocket dictionaries are no good for the job we have in mind and the dictionaries that are good enough, like the *Concise Oxford*, *Chambers's Twentieth Century* and *Webster's Collegiate*, are too big to have with you when you come upon a word you don't know when reading in a train or bus. The problem of remembering the words when you are within reach of a dictionary is, however, no different from that of remembering anything, any time, anywhere.

Arnold Bennett put it on record that he read a dictionary for about twenty minutes every day. He was a professional writer and words were therefore his trade. I am not suggesting that you set yourself the task of reading a dictionary for so many minutes every day, but I do suggest that browsing in a dictionary now and then will have beneficial effects upon your vocabulary development. To look upon a dictionary as a book to browse in implies a very different attitude from the first one I mentioned, i.e. looking on the dictionary as the final arbiter in orthographical or semantic arguments.

When you have reached the stage of regarding a dictionary as a book to browse in now and then, your attention will no doubt be drawn to the etymology of words. You will find many interesting and surprising things about that aspect of language. Here, for example, is a list of words all of which, some by devious routes, have come from the Latin word *manus* which means 'hand': *manacle, manage, mandate, manicure, maniple, manner, manoeuvre, manual, manufacture, manure, command, emancipate*. Now you may care to follow that up by seeing if you can find ten words in whose pedigree there appears the Latin word for 'foot' – *pes, pedis*. It will not be very difficult for you to find ten such words in the *Concise Oxford*, all with the syllable *ped* in them. The word *pawn*, with no such syllable in it, is also derived from that Latin root, but note while you are engaged in this little exercise that neither *pedlar* nor *pedagogue* has that derivation. The word *pedigree* is peculiar in this context. A nineteenth-century edition of *Webster's Dictionary* gives as the accepted derivation the French *par degrés* (step by step) but adds as a footnote: 'By some authorities this word is said to be derived from the French *pied-de-grue* (crane's foot) a name formerly applied to the heraldic genealogical trees from their form.' It was only while working on these tests that I learned these facts about 'pedigree' and a few days afterwards there appeared a book about the history of words in which *pied-de-grue* was accepted as the derivation. The title of the book was *Pedigree*.

Vocabulary and Intelligence

Is there any connection between extent of vocabulary and degree of intelligence? That question had long been at the back of my mind but I had pushed it aside because I do not feel at all comfortable with the term 'intelligence' nowadays. It has been so much tied up with IQs and so much bandied about in debates as to whether intelligence is innate or not that whenever I do use it in writing I feel like adding immediately after it a parenthetical qualifying paragraph.

It is for that kind of reason that many tests that were essentially the same as traditional intelligence tests have in recent years been called reasoning tests. In spite of the discomfort that the term generates in my mind, because that question about vocabulary and intelligence has been put to me several times recently, I feel I ought to try to answer it. Fortunately some direct statements can be made that need not involve anyone in hair-splitting arguments. For example, it is futile to begin to think of intelligence apart from behaviour. I do not mean by 'behaviour' merely physical actions, though most physical acts are accompanied, either as cause or effect, by intellectual and emotional events. More plainly, it is nonsense to speak of someone as being intelligent unless he or she has behaved in a manner that can be called intelligent. That would be like saying a man had a good mathematical intelligence who had never done any mathematical thinking or that a woman was a brilliant pianist whose only contact with a piano had been dusting the keys. It follows that the clues as to whether a person is intelligent or not will depend to a large extent on his environment, i.e. the complex of situations in which his behaviour takes place. The inhabitant of a rock-village high in the Andes will have a limited vocabulary but may act very intelligently within his environment. The village schoolmaster who taught me Latin had a vast English vocabulary but acted with little intelligence when it came to reversing his 7 h.p. car – unless you call it intelligent to make a round tour of twelve miles to avoid making a three-point turn. During this century our ideas about intelligence have been so closely linked with formal education in which books play a major role that we may have exaggerated the importance of linguistic behaviour as evidence of intelligence. Nevertheless, if we consider mental alertness and curiosity as signs of intelligence – and I think we must – then anyone who grows into adulthood in an environment where language is thrown so unremittingly at him by press, radio and television and yet does not acquire a substantial vocabulary has not shown much sign of mental alertness or curiosity.

Among educational psychologists it has long been accepted that vocabulary-rating is, as they put it, 'one of the best predictors of educability'. In an American university it had become a matter of routine to give student-entrants a series of tests. One of these was a short vocabulary test of twenty-nine words. An analysis of several years' results revealed that the scores in that short vocabulary test correlated more highly than any of the other scores with later success or failure in the courses of study. There seems in fact good reason for thinking that the possession of a large vocabulary indicates that a fair amount of intelligent behaviour has been going on. On the other hand a person who drifts through life in a society so largely dominated by words in speech and print without inquiring into the meanings of a large number of those words produces little evidence that under such a bushel of ignorance shines a dazzling intelligence.

Technical Terms

The tests in this book measure *general* vocabulary – that is to say, the number you finally arrive at will not give you credit for knowing highly technical terms or even dialect words. But, of course, there is no hard-and-fast dividing line between technical terms and the general vocabulary of a language nor indeed between dialect words and those of the general vocabulary.

The word 'technical' in this context is not as limited in meaning as it is in the name 'technical college', a place where you would not expect to find, for example, a 'poetry workshop' in operation. Yet poetry has its techniques and its technical terms. The first equivalent of *technical* given in the *Concise Oxford* is 'of or in a particular art, science, handicraft, etc.', and the first equivalent of *etc.* is given as 'and the rest'. You could hardly get a term with a wider connotation than that. We all know some technical terms connected with our jobs. Indeed without a fair sprinkling of technical terms we'd hardly have a vocabulary at all. That is why it is necessary to make the qualification '*highly* technical terms', i.e. those known to a comparatively small number of people because of their highly specialized knowledge of 'a particular art, science, handicraft, etc.'.

The word *jargon* could be used in this connection, for one of its equivalents (I quote *Webster's Collegiate Dictionary*) is 'the technical terminology or characteristic idiom of a special activity or group'. However, 'jargon' carries with it derogatory implications that are out of place here; 'confused unintelligible language' and 'obscure and often pretentious language marked by circumlocutions and long words' are two dictionary equivalents of 'jargon'. There is an older use of 'jargon', namely as a verb meaning 'to twitter' or 'to warble'. That is a use I can recall meeting only once, in *The Rime of the Ancient Mariner*:

> Sometimes a-dropping from the sky
> I heard the skylark sing;
> Sometimes all little birds that are,
> How they seemed to fill the sea and air
> With their sweet jargoning!

A word that can be described as a highly technical term one year may pass into the general vocabulary the next. Indeed most new words in this science-dominated age where specialization is a necessity begin as highly technical terms. Many remain in that category. A few come into the general vocabulary. 'Thalidomide' is one that came into the general vocabulary. Once it was a cold unit in the technical vocabularies of chemistry and medicine; now it is widely known and is heavily charged with the emotions that surround tragic events. Advertising can bring a highly technical term into the general vocabulary – 'polyurethane' is an example; it is fairly generally regarded now as the name of an ingredient in hard-surface paint. This word has not yet reached the main body of the *Concise Oxford*. Until a new edition is published it will stay among the few hundred words that appear in the section headed 'Addenda'.

It could be argued that a layman's knowledge of a term like 'polyurethane' is spurious. He goes into a hardware shop and asks for a tin of polyurethane paint but hasn't a notion of the chemical basis of the substance. True, but in that respect the term 'polyurethane' is no different from thousands of others that we use. What about 'inflation'? Does anybody who uses that once-technical term in economics know enough about the complex events behind the term, which give it its meaning, to cure this economic ill? Words are used with different levels of knowledge and at different levels of meaning. I have heard a physicist using the word 'work' as a technical term and as an ordinary day-to-day word both in the same sentence.

Dialect words sometimes have similar histories. I find the word 'dunt', which I knew as meaning 'a heavy blow' in a Scots dialect now used as a technical term in aeronautics signifying the bump that ensues when an aircraft hits an upward-rushing current of air.

As knowledge accumulates, so the vocabulary of a language increases. Men have to invent new names because they have discovered new things or new facts about things. Aristotle did not need much of a vocabulary to set down in writing what he knew about the brain because about all he knew about it was that it was there to cool the blood! So obviously it is possible to be a powerful thinker without knowing much about the thing you think with. Today it would be a fairly ignorant person who did not know more words connected with the brain than Aristotle did. A medical practitioner needs to know a fair number of technical terms relating to the brain and its functions and a neuro-surgeon needs more terms and a deeper knowledge of what lies behind the medical practitioner's terms. Most of us, however, can get along quite well without understanding a piece of writing like this:

The cornu ammonis is situated close to the medial wall of the inferior horn of the lateral ventrical. Since this wall of the hemisphere is thin, there is in the depth of the fissure hippocampi, a continuity between the cornu ammonis proper and the adjacent parts of the cortex, namely the narrow entorhinal and perirhinal formations which on the height of the gyrus hippocampi go over into the temporal area.

One of the purposes of technical language is to be precise so that the mind of the reader can remain fixed with exactness on the matter in hand, but, when I read that passage, at the back of my mind there appears a weird mountain landscape where horned antelopes buck and spring and where in grassy valleys wild horses facially resembling hippopotami safely graze.

Writing like that looks difficult, but only because of the heavy load of technical terms. If you were really familiar with those terms, that piece of writing would be no more difficult to read than this:

The historic tavern known as the Trip to Jerusalem is situated under the towering Castle Rock. The tourist can best reach it from the Old Market Square by way of Friar Lane . . .

The increasing load of vocabulary has become a problem in many branches of science. A few years ago this problem was felt with peculiar force in the science of entomology. In connection with this, the following comment appeared in the *New Scientist*:

Taxonomists, people whose concern is with discriminating between various species and the application of a logical system of animal names, have for long used the microscopic structure of the male insect sex organ and its adjacent copulatory hooks as the basis of insect identification. But the student of dragonflies knows little about ants, the waterbug specialist nothing of microlepidoptera. So there has arisen a fascinating but bewildering mass of technical terms used in describing male and female insect mating structure, some 2,000 or so names in Latin, English, French and German. Reduction of this mountain of terms requires two things, first a system of homologies between comparable parts of bug and beetle, moth and mosquito, secondly an agreed international terminology.

The comment went on to congratulate Dr S. L. Tuxen, an eminent Danish authority on silverfish and springtails, on managing to edit and get through the press in six and a half years a volume called *A Taxonomist's Glossary of Genitalia in Insects* to which thirty-four writers of many nationalities contributed.

That's the best instance I know of the problem of vocabulary in a science. You may think that pursuing the thing to these lengths is pedantic, and anticipating this, the author pointed out that insect taxonomy was the basis on which research into many important problems was erected and he gave as examples: premature coconut fall in the Solomons, the dreadful problem of native blindness in West Africa and damage to raspberries in central Scotland.

The question I had in mind in writing this section was: When is a term technical, highly technical, or not technical at all? What I have written shows that there isn't a hard-and-fast answer. The rule I adopted, with some misgivings, was that if the editors of the current editions of the dictionaries I used included a word, I could not regard that word as too highly technical for the literacy tests. The basis of the *Concise Oxford* was laid at a time when classical studies dominated higher education; so there still remain in the dictionary a fair number of terms referring to the technicalities of ancient Greek grammar and rhetoric that are too technical for words!

Our Daily Read: The Vocabulary of Newspapers

The British people have the reputation of being the most voracious readers of newspapers in the world. I thought it would be interesting, while my 'feel for the dictionary' was still sensitive, to measure the vocabularies of some newspapers against the scale set by the Standard Literacy Tests. I did this by finding in each of them the 100 words that in my judgment came highest in the Literacy Test Levels. A newspaper in which there were 100 words in the Levels 4–6 would, of course, demand a higher standard of literacy than one which would require a descent to Level 2 in order to fill the quota of 100.

Below I give the hundred most 'advanced' words in each of the newspapers analysed, arranged according to Levels. In the three newspapers that produce colour supplements the reading material in the supplements was not included, nor in any instance was the wording of advertisements. The *Sunday Mirror* had a longish medical article on the day I analysed it; that gave it a few extra points in the 'league table' I publish at the end of this section. I omitted two technical terms referring to types of cupressus in the *Daily Mail*; they were given in brackets and therefore not necessary for the understanding of the text. They would not have changed the positions in the 'league table', however.

The Times

Level 6   *amici curiae*, baguette, *caveat emptor*, *entrepôt*, *grisaille*, mandamus, *odium scholasticum*, polyptych, rifampicin, *salle des ventes*, seise, spandrel, tat-seller, tonne, *torchères*.

Total 15

Level 5   appellate, artefact, *bonne bouche*, boulevardier, bullish, cathode, cinégaste, denature, dexter, *évènements*, exegesis, fugal, ideogram, Ordovician, podium, pragmatic, scrip, Silurian, thermoluminescent, triptych.

Total 20

Level 4   abrogate, activism, actuarial, aegis, affinity, amnesty,
ancillary, anomaly, baroque, calibrate, cavort,
clandestine, consortium, debenture, demerit, desultory,
divisive, empirical, *époque*, equities, euphemism,
Eurocrat, expiation, extra-judicial, fiscal, flamboyance,
genre, gouache, gyration, ideological, imbalance,
incantation, indigence, interlocutory, jobber, laity,
liquidity, neobarbarism, notation, oestrogen, orgiastic,
palliative, penchant, predatory, prerogative, prescience,
psychedelic, rapport, rapprochement, rebut, recession,
reciprocity, reclamation, resilience, retroactive, salutory,
sporadic, subliminal, surveillance, tempera, trenchant,
variance, vignette, vociferous, Zeitgeist.

Total 65

No need for 'contributions' from Levels 1, 2, and 3 and
indeed not all the Level 4 words were used in making up the
100 most 'difficult' words.

Sunday Times

Level 6   agora, finocchio, lovage, *promenade en arabesque*,
'proette', theobromine.

Total 6

Level 5   androgynous, *catalogue raisonné*, chatelaine, epicene,
équilibre, frisson, myelin, polypropylene, surrogate.

Total 9

Level 4   alimony, ameliorate, analogy, ancillary, atrophied,
attrition, avant-garde, banality, barbiturate, basil,
carnality, cavil, chervil, choleric, clandestine, clemency,
coefficient, coitus, coma, *coup de théâtre*, cumulative,
débâcle, declamatory, dentated, depreciation, dill, diurnal,
ebullience, empathy, equivocal, erode, esoteric, euphoria,
evocation, extrapolation, forensic, furore, histrionic,
hysterectomy, indemnity, ineptitude, inexpugnable,
kickshaw, lachrymose, laconic, lexicon, luminary,
macro-economics, mandatory, mayhem, megalomania,
myopia, obligato, olfactory, placebo, pre-empt,

pretentious, prognostication, propitious, recondite,
reflationary, schizophrenia, scintillating, sclerosis,
scurrilous, seminar, serialism, simplicism, stockjobber,
succulent, tarragon, tautological, transvestism, trauma,
unequivocally, virulent.

Total 76

Level 3   beneficiary, clinical, competence, crucial, insidious,
insolvent, irrevocably, lithograph, participant.

Total 9

The Observer

Level 6   *concentracao*, *favela*, retsina.

Total 3

Level 5   aetiology, astral, bathetic, calcification, chota,
déjà vu, exegesis, *franglais*, gestalt, pansexual, pederasty,
stomatic, syphiophobe, teleology.

Total 14

Level 4   accreditation, attrition, baroque, bravado,
cadaverous, cauterize, cavort, chauvinist, collage, condone,
connivance, contingent, cravat, desiccating, deterrent,
disquisition, dissident, dossier, ebullience, élitist, ensemble,
entourage, episodic, exacerbating, exemplary, exhortation,
exorcize, expressionist, factorial, falsetto, felicitous,
fixated, habitué, ignominy, incumbent, insouciance,
interstice, intuitive, jingoized, kibbutz, liquidity, lobbying,
mandatory, meticulous, mien, nihilism, obsequious,
oeuvre, parlous, permeate, philistine, polemic, procedural,
recession, scalloped, sophism, sententious, solecism,
sporadic, surfeit, temerity, tirade, trauma, ubiquitous.

Total 64

Level 3   adroit, brusque, charlatan, exposition, extremism,
incipient, increment, inebriated, interim, labyrinthine,
liaison, manipulate, mulatto, pulverize, pyrotechnics,
referendum, sculpt, statutory, tribunal.

Total 19

Sunday Telegraph

Level 6   *dotation, iki-gai, moretacu-shain, uchi, zarzuela.*
> Total 5

Level 5   annuitant, cabriole, demonic, Diktat, *éminence grise*, horrendous, *kamikaze*, podium, *prêt à porter*, puissance, *rubato, succès de scandale*, transmogrification, troglodyte.
> Total 14

Level 4   abrasive, accoutrement, aura, autopsy, birdie, caddie, callipers, castigate, comatose, compulsive, contingency, contrition, convertibility, coverage, davenport, deflationary, dissimulate, durables, eclecticism, egocentric, enhancement, exemplar, fantasist, garrulity, grandiose, groundswell, haemorrhage, humanoid, hypochondria, incarcerate, incisive, incremental, ingratiate, interegna, jobber, limbo, merger, metamorphosis, moratorium, paranoid, parochialism, penalogical, penultimate, peripheral, peroration, plummet, preamble, replete, reportage, reversion, sonority, surreptitious, vagary, virulent.
> Total 54

Level 3   abortion, aspirant, assiduous, autonomy, barometric, bastion, bureaucracy, charlatanism, commitment, deference, epistolary, ersatz, extinction, glacial, graduated, idiom, inducement, labyrinthine, lucrative, lustre, orthodoxy, predatory, pollution, prerequisite, radical, reappraisal, relevant.
> Total 27

Three of the Level 6 words here are Japanese. The meanings were indicated in English in the article.

Daily Telegraph

Level 6   *aegrotat, mantra.*
> Total 2

Level 5   apothegm, arthritic, *Ostpolitik*, paraplegic.
> Total 4

Level 4   *adagio*, agrotechnologist, *allegro*, archives, archivist,
augury, bizarre, buttressed, calibre, circa, claustrophobic,
cliché, coloratura, consortium, contingency, croûton,
demonic, *détente*, differential, discretionary, effluent,
empathy, emolument, entrepreneurship, erasure, ethic,
expertise, explicit, felicitous, fortuitous, faction, foreclose,
gauche, *grand guignol*, hermaphrodite, hormone,
impeachment, implicit, inhalation, instigate, insular,
inundated, invoice, malaise, meticulous, misconstrue,
monitor, obdurate, palliative, parity, plethora, poundage,
precept, proctor, psychopath, quantify, rateable,
recuperative, repository, resilience, reticence, revert,
sado-masochistic, salutary, schizophrenia, sclerosis,
Shintoism, sinuous, surety, surrogate, surveillance,
tarragon, therapy, trauma, triumvirate, vicissitude.

Total 76

Level 3   acquisition, catastrophic, commitment, corruption,
devastating, indelibly, momentum, posture, regionalism,
retrospective, ritual, riveting, speculation, statutory,
subsidiary, technique, trait, zenith.

Total 18

The Guardian

Level 6   eponymous, ergonomist, odometer.

Total 3

Level 5   chordal, declination, foliated, gestalt, *glissando*,
micron, reliquary, triptych, voyeuristic, *vis comica*.

Total 10

Level 4   additive, alignment, bizarre, bucolic, caries, ceramic,
choreography, circumspect, conceptualize, depredation,
draconian, egregious, electro-therapy, emanate, ethereal,
ethnic, fabricator, filigree, fiscal, Gothic, hypothetical,
ideological, implication, inordinately, intransigent,
irrevocable, junketing, liquidity, litigation, liturgy,
Luddite, marital, matrix, militancy, mutant, multilateral,
novitiate, nuance, plenitude, predatory, sacrosanct,
sardonic, semi-conductor, socio-economic, spectrometer,
spillage, streptomycin, sucrose, tangible, tempo, thesis,
thrombosis, virtuosity.

Total 53

Level 3   accession, aesthetic, anthology, assessment,
    authenticity, authorization, bogus, concession, credible,
    crucial, curricula, deprivation, diaphragm, disrupt,
    dynamic, expediency, incongruous, innate, innovation,
    interim, levy, monetary, organic, oxygenated, patriarch,
    pedantic, potential, propagation, scholastic, spectrum,
    tariff, textile, vestige, zenith.

                                                    Total 34

    No need for any words from Levels 1 and 2.

Sunday Express

Level 6   amphigoric, myoclonic, quenelle, subreption,
    tryptophan.

                                                    Total 5

Level 5   pawpaw, pomander.

                                                    Total 2

Level 4   amino-acid, arterio-sclerosis, aubergine, basil,
    bizarre, burgeon, capsicum, chauvinist, coagulation,
    collage, consortium, cuisine, dilation,
    electro-encephalograph, escargot, expertise, guava,
    guddle, hassle, haemorrhage, hermaphrodite, hernia,
    hibiscus, holocaust, integral, leukaemia, lichee,
    meticulous, ophthalmoscope, pasta, preamble, prestigious,
    psychosomatic, retina, scuffed, strident, succulent,
    thrombosis, turquoise.

                                                    Total 39

Level 3   adamant, allegation, aloofness, amenable, assignment,
    audition, balustrade, bilateral, boggle, buffoon, busker,
    calorie, category, chagrin, circuit, clinch, commodity,
    debut, dilation, directive, discipline, dossier, egotistical,
    escort, evict, extort, fastidious, flotilla, hone, identifiable,
    idiom, immaculate, indefatigable, indolent, inflatable,
    inscrutable, iris, irrational, jeopardize, longevity, malign,
    mosaic, nonchalant, objective, obsession, opt, opulent,
    pandemonium, poignant, pomegranate, potential, prodigy,
    prolific, psychic.

                                                    Total 54

Daily Mail

Level 6   tufa.

Total 1

Level 5   camellia, chiaroscuro, courgette, cupressus,
dexomyphitamine, langouste, tine, vesicular.

Total 8

Level 4   acrimony, adherence, affidavit, alienate, annul,
apathetic, cannabis, chef d'oeuvre, columnar, co-ordinate,
consortium, contravene, coverage, coypu, cuisine, federal,
foray, forsythia, gourmet, haulm, ignoble, ignominious,
integral, kaput, laminated, periphery, perjury, polemicist,
prodigality, ratify, recession, sadistic, sinuous, teeter,
telex, translucent, versatility, writ.

Total 38

Level 3   access, breach, clamp, compensation, conifer,
contaminate, context, crucial, derelict, diminution, evict,
exotic, facilities, floral, herbaceous, hurly-burly, gesture,
identity, inducement, inflation, ingredient, intensive,
investment, irretrievable, itinerary, lavish, liability,
marginal, musquash, obliterate, obsolete, palate,
phenomenal, phosphorescence, polyanthus, precocity,
reclamation, signify, specify, sponsor, statutory,
substantial, successive, superlative, surcharge, tacit,
technique, tenure, transcript, vandalism, verve, wastage,
zealous.

Total 53

Sunday Mirror

Level 6   laparotomy.

Total 1

Level 5   odontoid, plesiosaur.

Total 2

Level 4   acupuncture, allergic, appendectomy, asphyxiate, astringent, backdrop, bizarre, brokerage, capitalize, clique, compulsive, defunct, degradation, dermatologist, dossier, enormity, franchise, guise, histamine, improvisation, inveterate, kebab, klaxon, laconically, macabre, migraine, neurosis, pathologist, pizza, plasma, prevaricate, sedative, synchronize, tedium, tenuous, therapy, undulate, vigilante.

Total 38

Level 3   abdominal, agonizing, alleviate, analysis, apparition, aversion, blitz, bracketed, buttonholing, chiffon, clinical, compensation, decisive, dedication, deprivation, detachable, diabolical, diagnose, dignitary, dilemma, eventually, facial, ferocity, focus, foreboding, foundered, hallucination, harrowing, incautious, incompetence, infamous, integrity, legislation, lynch, marginal, massive, outlandish, pallor, participant, perennial, petulant, potential, priority, prototype, purge, registerable, requisite, rudiments, saunter, scourge, self-denial, statistics, stiletto, tariff, terminate, tripod.

Total 56

Level 2   chaos, unendurable, vehicle.

Total 3

Daily Express

Level 6   None.

Level 5   surrogate.

Total 1

Level 4   apartheid, candour, coma, co–ordination, coverage, dressage, episcopate, faction, frigidity, gaffe, grapevine, iguana, impotence, inertia, infiltrate, integral, integrity, introvert, intrusion, maestro, meretricious, perjury, pervert, psychopath, punitive, schizophrenic, secrete, surety, terrain.

Total 29

Level 3   adamant, aggregate, allege, atrocity, attributable,
automation, callous, canine, capability, category,
cavalcade, charter, circuit, clearance, colleague,
committal, commitment, controversial, crucial,
debauchery, delinquency, diabetic, dilemma, disrupt,
dissuade, dubious, duplicate, effective, ego, erupt,
evaluate, eviction, fanatical, frigate, frustration,
germinate, guidance, hypnotize, indecision, ingredient,
inflated, intensive, intervention, involvement, legendary,
medication, militancy, naïve, oust, posture, precinct,
promotion, provision, psychiatrist, puritanical, radiant,
radius, reaction, recipient, reduction, reinstate, revert,
sedative, solar, strategist, succour, suspension, tribunal,
valuation, vaudeville.

Total 70

News of the World

Level 6   *fattura.*

Total 1

Level 5   hemiplegia, surrogate, up-tempo.

Total 3

Level 4   abomination, bizarre, colleen, diamante, faction,
finesse, hepatitis, lacerate, malpractice, parapsychology,
psychometry, psychopath, therapy.

Total 13

Level 3   abduction, accentuate, affable, alibi, allege,
antagonism, arrogance, awesome, bacteria, clairvoyance,
clinical, commute, compassionate, compère, compromise,
concede, conformist, contagious, curvaceous, dedication,
demolition, deterrent, discreet, disruption, eliminate,
erotic, evaporate, exclusion, extensive, extravaganza,
facet, fanatic, forte, frustration, gesture, graft,
identification, illogical, impotent, ironically, medallion,
neutral, oblivious, obsession, optimum, outrage, pillory,
provocation, poignant, potential, prefabricate, prosecution,
rapist, realistic, repulsive, resignation, respiration,

revelation, rummage, seduce, septuagenarian,
sophisticated, sponsor, strenuous, stylish, subtlety,
superlative, suppress, syndicate, tension, testimony,
textile, tiara, ultimate, unimpeachable, unrepentant,
unscrupulous, vane, vested, vindication, vindictive, virus,
voodoo.

Total 83

Daily Mirror

Level 6   None.

Level 5   None.

Level 4   amnesty, aural, evangelic, hormone, hysterectomy,
militancy, nutrient, prurient, resilient, searing, stigma,
surveillance, temerity, transvestite, viperish.

Total 15

Level 3   advisory, alienate, anaemia, anguish, articulately,
cancellation, castration, cocaine, confection, consecutive,
controversial, crucial, custody, delinquency, dilemma,
diminution, discrimination, disharmony, enforce, fervour,
foil, formal, gaggle, genitals, giblets, hesitancy,
homosexuality, intuition, ingredient, juggernaut, legality,
paprika, posture, potential, prestige, provision,
psychiatrist, restructure, revivify, slatternly, slouch,
subsidiary, subtlety, tension, uncannily.

Total 45

Level 2   ailment, allege, alternative, area, barricade,
beneficial, campaigner, cassette, challenge, collapse,
compulsory, concentration, consumption, convert,
demonstration, depressed, electrify, expose, freak,
gravity, indignant, minimum, pacifist, prejudice, scheme,
spectacle, squad, standard, stationary, subject, surpass,
terminate, thug, traditional, unacceptable, undignified,
universal, vehicle, warehouse, warrant.

Total 40

Level 6   Bornholm disease, devil's grip.

Total 2

Level 5   dermabrasion, holography.

Total 2

Level 4   autopsy, axe-man, bizarre, cannabis, coven, exorcism, laser, macabre, machete, marcel, occult, spey.

Total 12

Level 3   aggregate, allegation, avert, bludgeon, brusque, calibre, chicory, chronological, controversy, deteriorate, disciplinary, drawbridge, dynamic, entourage, erratic, fracas, ghoulish, integrity, intestines, maestro, marijuana, narcotic, perpetrate, poignant, potential, premature, relevant, sponsor, status, swashbuckling, tenacity, tenure, tuba.

Total 33

Level 2   absorbing, access, achieve, appeal, average, booking, breath-taking, burgle, caution, challenge, cockpit, concentrate, correspondence, diet, disapprove, disgraceful, encounter, energy, ebb, elegant, extend, frequent, glamour, ideal, influential, league, legion, ludicrous, merit, obstinate, official, protective, portray, practise, publicity, qualify, reception, relentless, resent, reward, salary, selection, stubborn, tackle, temporary, thunderbolt, tournament, transfer, trek, unrivalled, veteran.

Total 51

The Sun

Level 6   None.

Level 5   None.

Level 4   None.

Level 3   abduct, accost, allegation, animated, assets,
back-bencher, bird-brained, blatantly, cartilage, classical,
compensation, concede, confrontation, corruption,
debutante, defraud, deprive, enviable, erupt, estranged,
evasive, expectancy, fascism, firebrand, foil, grotesque,
grouch, incur, innuendo, intrigue, lottery, niggling,
oracle, outrageous, questionable, picket, policy,
precarious, product, qualms, reconcile, seizure, sequence,
sequinned, skittish, sponsor, tactics, tipster, turmoil,
vibrant.

Total 50

Level 2   ambassador, antic, bankrupt, barrier, bribery,
campaign, cancellation, carnival, commercial,
compulsory, drab, equipment, essential, excavator,
export, forger, generate, genuine, hardship, hazardous,
hibernate, hitch, identity, involve, mammoth, marathon,
massive, memoir, misguided, mystified, offensive,
opponent, post-mark, post-mortem, potential, precaution,
ransom, release, reluctant, representative, safeguard,
security, specialist, spectacular, speculation, stadium,
stake, vicious, warder.

Total 49

Literacy League Table

Level	6	5	4	3	2	Total
The Times	6×15 90	5×20 100	4×65 260			450
Sunday Times	6×6 36	5×9 45	4×76 304	3×9 27		412
The Observer	6×3 18	5×14 70	4×64 256	3×19 57		401
Sunday Telegraph	6×5 30	5×14 70	4×54 216	3×27 81		397
Daily Telegraph	6×2 12	5×4 20	4×76 304	3×18 54		390

The Guardian	6×3 18	5×10 50	4×53 212	3×34 102		382
Sunday Express	6×5 30	5×2 10	4×39 156	3×54 162		358
Daily Mail	6×1 6	5×8 40	4×38 152	3×53 159		357
Sunday Mirror	6×1 6	5×2 10	4×38 152	3×56 168	2×3 6	342
Daily Express	6×0 0	5×1 5	4×29 116	3×70 210		331
News of the World	6×1 6	5×3 15	4×13 52	3×83 249		322
Daily Mirror	6×0 0	5×0 0	4×15 60	3×45 135	2×40 80	275
The Sunday People	6×2 12	5×2 10	4×12 48	3×33 99	2×51 102	271
The Sun	6×0 0	5×0 0	4×0 0	3×50 150	2×49 98	248

Circulation and Vocabulary

The Times which heads the Literacy League Table is at the bottom of the list when the national dailies are listed according to the circulation figures. It would be very rash, however, to deduce from that fact the generalization that the lighter the vocabulary load of a newspaper is the bigger its circulation will be. Things don't work out as tidily as that. The editor who is beset by circulation problems will not solve them by insisting that his staff study the Standard Literacy Tests and take care never to use a word that does not qualify to be in Levels 1 or 2. A comparison of the *Daily Telegraph* and the *Guardian* is to the point here. Circulation figures issued in 1973 showed the *Daily Telegraph* as having a daily sale of nearly one and a half million and the *Guardian* as below 400,000. Yet my sample showed the *Telegraph* as having a heavier vocabulary load than the *Guardian*.

Clearly, other factors than vocabulary load influence the circulation figures. It might even be argued that vocabulary is not a factor in determining circulation at all – which is very much like saying that a hybrid paper with *Times* reading matter and *Sun* pictures would sell as well as the *Sun*. That experiment is unlikely ever to be tried.

In any case I am not putting forward the Literacy League Table as a significant contribution to the sociological study of the press. A full analysis would naturally take into account the amount of reading matter in the various papers. There are obviously fewer words in a tabloid with double-spread illustrations and display headlines than in the closer-set *Times* or *Daily Telegraph*. My analysis of newspaper vocabularies was no more than an interesting sideline to the main business of vocabulary measurement. Everybody knows that the most popular newspapers make smaller demands on vocabulary than the 'heavies' – but something interesting does emerge from the simple analysis and it is that no newspaper is written for semi-literates. That is a vague term in its normal usage, often indeed a term of abuse. I would define it here as signifying an adult who has difficulty in reading and whose vocabulary as measured by the Standard Literacy Tests does not go much beyond 10,000 words. The *Sun* in the randomly selected issue that I analysed contained among its hundred most 'difficult' words 50 at Level 3, i.e. at the 18,000-word level. Yet I have no doubt that the *Sun* is bought and enjoyed by many people whose vocabularies do not exceed 12,000 words. The fact is that newspapers are not *studied*: politicians read editorials, political commentaries, parliamentary reports, and so on; sports addicts probably turn first to the sports pages; women may read the fashion and heartache pages – and all those who have no reading or vocabulary problems at least glance at the general interest news items and features. A comparatively small number of people do not go much further than the pictures and the comic strips.

Newspapers of the English-Speaking World

A vast acreage of newsprint pours from the presses every day. A vast acreage of forest is laid low every day in order to keep those presses supplied. It would take a full research team well endowed with funds and time to produce a scientific report on the newspapers of the English-speaking world alone. In the matter of vocabulary, however, I strongly doubt whether in the end they would come up with anything very different from what I found from a small sample. The chief fact that emerged is that there is a quite remarkable similarity between newspapers in all parts of the English-speaking world in the range of vocabulary used. In the tabloid type of newspaper you are likely to find a bigger proportion of local idioms and colloquialisms but apart from these the vocabulary is very much that of the *Sunday People* or the *Sun*. Those newspapers, however, which according to their lights offer serious political comment, would appear somewhere between the *Daily Telegraph* and the *Daily Mail* in my Literacy League Table. Examples of such newspapers are: in Australia, *The Australian* and the *Sydney Morning Herald*; in Canada, the *Vancouver Sun*, the Toronto *Globe and Mail* and the *Star*, and the *Star* of Montreal; in South Africa, the *Cape Times* and the *Rand Daily Mail*; in New Zealand, *The Dominion*. There are, I have no doubt, many others in those countries. Those I have named are newspapers of which I have examined recent copies or of which I have previous knowledge.

The press of America is a colossus. I once read how many square miles of timber had to be cut to supply the newsprint for the Sunday editions alone. It was an incredible figure, but unfortunately it was also forgettable. If any Briton prides himself on the undoubted fact that more newspapers come into the average British home than into average homes anywhere else in the world, he might well give some thought to the fact that if all the Sunday papers of Britain were put in one bundle, that bundle would not be as big as the Sunday edition of the *New York Times*.

The compactness of Great Britain compared with the huge sprawl of the United States has led to a big difference in the structure of the press in the two countries. We have national newspapers and these are unknown in the United States. The part that the *Washington Post* played in the Watergate affair probably turned it into something like a national newspaper for a few months, but normally the nearest approach to national coverage is to be found in the syndicated columns of the top political and social columnists. In Britain no matter where you live you find the local newsagents carrying the same newspapers, some of them with regional variations, but all stamped with the same editorial hall-mark. The American magazine *Time*, though not in the ordinary sense a newspaper, is probably as near to nation-wide as you can get in American journalism. I examined a copy of it and found that its vocabulary load was somewhat less than that of the *Sunday Express*; there were only two words in that issue that I had not encountered in current British English – *bimbo* and *epoxied*. *Bimbo* does not appear among the 152,337 'entries' of *Webster's New Collegiate Dictionary* and *epoxied* is given as 'glued with epoxy resin'. A few words that I knew the meaning of in ordinary contexts puzzled me. I read, for example, that one of the chefs in the White House resigned partly because he was tired of serving Lyndon Johnson with 'spoon bread'. I took that to be bread-and-butter pudding and was not far wrong for according to Webster spoon bread is 'soft bread made with cornmeal mixed with eggs, milk and shortening and served with a spoon'. A similar difficulty with 'hang gliders' in the New Zealand *Dominion* was not so easily solved for I did not have a dictionary of New Zealand usage at hand or perhaps it was merely that I was short in my aeronautical vocabulary. I was interested, however, to find, again in Webster, that one of the American meanings of *glider* is 'a porch seat suspended from an upright framework by short chains or straps'.

I would have put the word *caucus* in Level 4 but found from the *Australian* that it would be a Level 3 word in that country since it occurred seven times in the first column in the term 'Labor Caucus'.

This is a book about vocabulary. It may give the erroneous impression that vocabulary load is the cause of difficult reading, but I. A. Richards translated Plato's *Republic* into Basic English, and there are some complicated ideas there. A less elevated example: Have you ever heard people arguing about the meaning of this simple sentence:

> Brothers and sisters have I none,
> but that man's father is my father's son.

Test No. 1

Level 1
1. abroad
2. binoculars
3. daily
4. expedition
5. horizon
6. jangle
7. limit
8. pattern
9. rate
10. stroke

Level 2
11. abandon
12. ballot
13. chaos
14. contraband
15. excavate
16. fatigue
17. laboratory
18. manual
19. purchase
20. shuttle

Level 3
21. abridge
22. aggregate
23. bivouac
24. chronology
25. credulous
26. hireling
27. indolent
28. meagre
29. nomadic
30. occidental

Level 4
31. abhorrent
32. amorphous
33. crustacean
34. declivity
35. emaciated
36. fabrication
37. galaxy
38. heretical
39. igneous
40. nomenclature

Level 5
41. abscissa
42. badinage
43. cartel
44. daemon
45. dendrite
46. exordium
47. inchoate
48. moraine
49. rubric
50. soutane

Level 6
51. aboulia
52. bicuspid
53. caracole
54. chalybeate
55. croton
56. dysphoria
57. gazebo
58. kymograph
59. ortolan
60. quadrat

Test No. 2

Level 1	Level 2	Level 3
1 abbey	11 accelerate	21 acrid
2 abundance	12 aquatic	22 aftermath
3 boast	13 celebrity	23 centrifugal
4 convenience	14 identical	24 circuitous
5 decimal	15 laboratory	25 faction
6 hazardous	16 latitude	26 interim
7 limit	17 martial	27 nautical
8 somersault	18 teem	28 retrograde
9 tuft	19 terminus	29 splice
10 undergrowth	20 veteran	30 vehement

Level 4	Level 5	Level 6
31 baroque	41 abreact	51 acronym
32 cabal	42 atavistic	52 breastsummer
33 Charybdis	43 claque	53 bronze
34 dorsal	44 dharma	54 dolmen
35 ephemeral	45 flagellum	55 eleemosynary
36 fiscal	46 gerrymander	56 gabbro
37 invective	47 haptic	57 ichthyolite
38 lymphatic	48 imbroglio	58 lycopod
39 mandible	49 janissary	59 maulstick
40 palliative	50 phrenetic	60 remora

Test No. 3

Level 1	Level 2	Level 3
1 absence	11 abode	21 acquisition
2 agriculture	12 barricade	22 alabaster
3 blizzard	13 bulletin	23 bigotry
4 crescent	14 climax	24 circumvent
5 downpour	15 crouch	25 culminate
6 fragment	16 export	26 fallacious
7 hemisphere	17 flimsy	27 mediocre
8 rigid	18 hospitality	28 nutritious
9 sheaf	19 longitude	29 parry
10 triangle	20 rustic	30 rancour

Level 4	Level 5	Level 6
31 acquiesce	41 accidie	51 boyar
32 agrarian	42 burette	52 catechumen
33 bullion	43 contumely	53 cudbear
34 clandestine	44 coruscate	54 dunnock
35 desultory	45 desuetude	55 fungible
36 eradicate	46 frustum	56 glabrous
37 flange	47 haulm	57 ocellus
38 homogeneous	48 imago	58 paxwax
39 laryngeal	49 mandragora	59 puisne
40 overt	50 normative	60 sciolist

Test No. 4

Level 1
1 accent
2 bough
3 curiosity
4 energetic
5 extinguish
6 grudge
7 ponder
8 quarter
9 surf
10 thrice

Level 2
11 abrupt
12 alternative
13 bisect
14 conspiracy
15 exploit
16 fathomless
17 lapse
18 rummage
19 sheer
20 stampede

Level 3
21 abolition
22 affluent
23 annex
24 beige
25 chafe
26 dank
27 epoch
28 labyrinth
29 mollusc
30 precipitate

Level 4
31 abrade
32 bizarre
33 cadence
34 deflation
35 evanescent
36 impeccable
37 obdurate
38 oligarchy
39 precursor
40 rotund

Level 5
41 acanthus
42 chimera
43 corvée
44 detritus
45 fontanelle
46 Georgic
47 integument
48 meniscus
49 phylactery
50 rhizome

Level 6
51 bathybius
52 cambium
53 deodand
54 electuary
55 futhorc
56 gesso
57 kiddle
58 nyctitropism
59 pledget
60 rodomontade

Test No. 5

Level 1
1 alter
2 barometer
3 distinct
4 festival
5 hardship
6 harpoon
7 matinée
8 reign
9 report
10 waste

Level 2
11 beverage
12 cardinal
13 demolish
14 graph
15 humdrum
16 impulsive
17 memorial
18 parallel
19 terminate
20 vivacious

Level 3
21 biography
22 decarbonize
23 domicile
24 facet
25 impunity
26 lore
27 mercenary
28 phantasm
29 restive
30 taboo

Level 4
31 actuate
32 bravura
33 comber
34 gouache
35 hieroglyphic
36 hybrid
37 iconoclast
38 maelstrom
39 muezzin
40 resurgent

Level 5
41 antinomy
42 carronade
43 dithyrambic
44 hebdomadal
45 infusoria
46 linage
47 medusa
48 myrmidon
49 paradigm
50 topology

Level 6
51 antonomasia
52 cartouche
53 dortour
54 elvan
55 filemot
56 isomer
57 lasher
58 noumenon
59 pulvinate
60 velleity

Test No. 6

Level 1
1 amusement
2 discipline
3 hollow
4 immense
5 macaroni
6 performance
7 radiator
8 repeat
9 tackle
10 uniform

Level 2
11 crusade
12 deposit
13 eclipse
14 humid
15 interfere
16 landmark
17 obstruct
18 rural
19 salvage
20 veterinary

Level 3
21 dexterity
22 expediency
23 expel
24 gravity
25 intersect
26 malefactor
27 medley
28 tranquillity
29 verdict
30 zenith

Level 4
31 anathema
32 encomium
33 incipient
34 juridical
35 leit-motif
36 morphology
37 ostensible
38 parabola
39 sargasso
40 torsion

Level 5
41 argot
42 bistre
43 etiolated
44 hierophant
45 ichnolite
46 kohlrabi
47 llano
48 objurgate
49 raddle
50 roulade

Level 6
51 bora
52 demurrer
53 hispid
54 kilderkin
55 logion
56 magma
57 operculum
58 riprap
59 samite
60 xylophagous

Test No. 7

Level 1
1 capital
2 centipede
3 diary
4 hibernate
5 hover
6 ledge
7 medium
8 pioneer
9 wobble
10 yelp

Level 2
11 curfew
12 gully
13 ignorance
14 laborious
15 merriment
16 obtainable
17 ravenous
18 rivet
19 temporary
20 visualize

Level 3
21 colossus
22 grapple
23 humiliate
24 invertebrate
25 lunar
26 mosaic
27 penance
28 sieve
29 tenacious
30 venomous

Level 4
31 capillary
32 genre
33 heterodox
34 jurisdiction
35 laminated
36 matrix
37 onus
38 parvenu
39 prehensile
40 sirocco

Level 5
41 atropine
42 diacritical
43 heterodyne
44 hubris
45 jalousie
46 lumen
47 metempsychosis
48 pointillist
49 provenance
50 semantic

Level 6
51 chiasmus
52 dipnoan
53 glaucous
54 ichthyornis
55 laniary
56 primage
57 reremouse
58 scantling
59 thanatology
60 ulema

Test No. 8

Level 1

1 apology
2 cartoon
3 easel
4 menace
5 naturalist
6 parachute
7 preparation
8 quarry
9 target
10 twilight

Level 2

11 ballet
12 bouquet
13 clamp
14 gnarled
15 landowner
16 operator
17 partition
18 rebellion
19 tacky
20 ventilation

Level 3

21 broach
22 capstan
23 gradient
24 languor
25 paramount
26 ravine
27 sequence
28 tundra
29 visa
30 warp

Level 4

31 fulminate
32 gambit
33 ignominy
34 leveret
35 lieu
36 mangrove
37 mellifluous
38 nexus
39 percept
40 rebut

Level 5

41 hecatomb
42 laager
43 motet
44 peccary
45 raceme
46 sacerdotal
47 squamous
48 tensor
49 verso
50 yellowback

Level 6

51 calamite
52 dugong
53 ecdysis
54 heriot
55 meuse
56 olibanum
57 pomace
58 sclerotic
59 tylopodous
60 uphroe

Test No. 9

Level 1	Level 2	Level 3
1 expert	11 extract	21 biped
2 gigantic	12 landscape	22 cartography
3 label	13 misinform	23 decrepit
4 limb	14 planetary	24 gregarious
5 medical	15 populous	25 interpolate
6 rascal	16 preservation	26 literacy
7 safety	17 recreation	27 niggardly
8 thatch	18 sample	28 parasite
9 trespass	19 tepid	29 upstart
10 volcano	20 vanity	30 volatile

Level 4	Level 5	Level 6
31 assonance	41 anemometer	51 boutade
32 gnomon	42 barouche	52 cloisonné
33 godwit	43 calenture	53 defeasance
34 philology	44 eozoic	54 emblements
35 prognosis	45 fricative	55 fermeture
36 querulous	46 lockage	56 limation
37 reciprocal	47 metathesis	57 melton
38 tarn	48 patristic	58 orgeat
39 unimpeachable	49 radix	59 rataplan
40 vacillation	50 ungulate	60 umiak

Test No. 10

Level 1
1 explosion
2 impatient
3 kangaroo
4 pirate
5 prowl
6 referee
7 slant
8 solo
9 unique
10 waste

Level 2
11 fledgling
12 hatchet
13 impact
14 javelin
15 landlubber
16 novelist
17 primitive
18 renown
19 tradition
20 urban

Level 3
21 cosmopolitan
22 diverge
23 interpose
24 lateral
25 niche
26 porous
27 rampant
28 territory
29 voodoo
30 yeoman

Level 4
31 ecology
32 laconic
33 linden
34 maxilla
35 paragon
36 prolixity
37 redolent
38 stertorous
39 timbre
40 vellum

Level 5
41 asymptotic
42 burlap
43 echidna
44 henry
45 interfacial
46 jeton
47 paregoric
48 rachitic
49 tanager
50 syncretism

Level 6
51 bisque
52 colporteur
53 decuman
54 grallatorial
55 isomorphous
56 orc
57 parataxis
58 riviere
59 tanagra
60 urticant

Test No. 11

Level 1

1 bandage
2 cashier
3 confectioner
4 extinguish
5 hobble
6 link
7 manufacture
8 overhead
9 pendulum
10 weight

Level 2

11 adverb
12 desolate
13 geometry
14 illegible
15 inattentive
16 jackal
17 lasso
18 mansion
19 oasis
20 pamphlet

Level 3

21 adjutant
22 barnacle
23 circumflex
24 decode
25 dispense
26 fluctuate
27 indestructible
28 patron
29 quirk
30 rankle

Level 4

31 actuarial
32 bas-relief
33 bowdlerize
34 canard
35 decibel
36 gasket
37 immanent
38 jacinth
39 patrimony
40 saturnine

Level 5

41 banzai
42 cateran
43 diopter
44 gasteropod
45 histology
46 pensile
47 sanserif
48 top-sawyer
49 transilient
50 ululate

Level 6

51 adytum
52 banderol
53 capitular
54 gallimaufry
55 hilding
56 imbricate
57 parergon
58 quincunz
59 sainfoin
60 vibraculum

Test No. 12

Level 1

1 extravagant
2 industry
3 litter
4 menagerie
5 pavilion
6 repetition
7 shudder
8 torch
9 vacant
10 whimper

Level 2

11 classic
12 discordant
13 fanfare
14 incubate
15 keel
16 locate
17 outwit
18 privilege
19 rectangle
20 sequel

Level 3

21 dialect
22 hostage
23 ingenuous
24 ingratiate
25 magnate
26 neutral
27 passive
28 pinion
29 supersede
30 velocity

Level 4

31 bifurcate
32 gaffe
33 incidence
34 junker
35 liturgy
36 marsupial
37 obsequious
38 pristine
39 rapprochement
40 sibilant

Level 5

41 anodyne
42 barton
43 cinquecento
44 galliard
45 glacis
46 isocheim
47 lallation
48 maenad
49 patristic
50 scutage

Level 6

51 agio
52 bolometer
55 chance-medley
54 epact
55 glyptics
56 jerque
57 labret
58 marquois
59 pappus
60 usufruct

Test No. 13

Level 1
1. ally
2. alphabetical
3. bracket
4. captive
5. dazzle
6. entertainment
7. nervous
8. panda
9. rogue
10. umpire

Level 2
11. client
12. oblique
13. parapet
14. oppression
15. skill
16. unity
17. well-to-do
18. whet
19. whiff
20. yolk

Level 3
21. chameleon
22. commodious
23. nonchalant
24. obsolete
25. option
26. primeval
27. silhouette
28. slogan
29. taciturn
30. yoke

Level 4
31. antithesis
32. neologism
33. nepotism
34. palpable
35. polonaise
36. rhombus
37. spindrift
38. umbrage
39. wainscot
40. wormwood

Level 5
41. chitinous
42. ecumenical
43. factitious
44. groundling
45. osillade
46. palimpsest
47. serendipity
48. shallop
49. umlaut
50. wapentake

Level 6
51. caracal
52. eirenicon
53. encrinite
54. nepanthe
55. od
56. pannage
57. razzia
58. screeve
59. umbra
60. wentletrap

Test No. 14

Level 1	Level 2	Level 3
1 amateur	11 aerated	21 atoll
2 attic	12 auction	22 butt
3 breadth	13 circumference	23 counterfeit
4 buffet	14 index	24 erratic
5 clutch	15 latter	25 fluorescent
6 monk	16 level	26 inconspicuous
7 munch	17 manoeuvre	27 isobar
8 record	18 plateau	28 jeopardy
9 smoulder	19 sensational	29 legion
10 zip	20 valour	30 spasmodic

Level 4	Level 5	Level 6
31 burgeon	41 anode	51 arrack
32 entente	42 catafalque	52 bulla
33 hyssop	43 holystone	53 cringle
34 introit	44 incunabula	54 lamia
35 jurisprudence	45 jejune	55 misprision
36 moratorium	46 lenitive	56 nano
37 napalm	47 melanism	57 repoussé
38 pastiche	48 peon	58 rundale
39 simian	49 seersucker	59 sutler
40 unequivocal	50 terrapin	60 water-gall

Test No. 15

Level 1
1 ballad
2 canoe
3 external
4 icicle
5 lame
6 magazine
7 martyr
8 mass
9 patriot
10 patrol

Level 2
11 abyss
12 bale
13 canyon
14 exterminate
15 instrument
16 lizard
17 obvious
18 password
19 rhythm
20 stoppage

Level 3
21 adaptable
22 capsule
23 daub
24 embargo
25 gargoyle
26 justify
27 liberate
28 memento
29 naturalize
30 oblivion

Level 4
31 calculus
32 debouch
33 gargantuan
34 ibid
35 laissez-faire
36 literati
37 neurology
38 obloquy
39 patois
40 rabid

Level 5
41 aclinic
42 banshee
43 illation
44 kelson
45 lachrymal
46 martingale
47 newton
48 occipital
49 petrology
50 ratlins

Level 6
51 babbitry
52 calumet
53 dehiscent
54 gault
55 hypocaust
56 kenosis
57 knap
58 limnology
59 mithridatism
60 unau

Test No. 16

Level 1
1 cloudless
2 invalid
3 laundry
4 model
5 pillion
6 recover
7 sculptor
8 steeple
9 tourist
10 witness

Level 2
11 carnivorous
12 exclude
13 highwayman
14 interpreter
15 litre
16 moderate
17 official
18 reduction
19 supreme
20 tournament

Level 3
21 item
22 lavish
23 maxim
24 pivot
25 ream
26 reputable
27 stigma
28 terminal
29 vagrant
30 yodel

Level 4
31 biretta
32 candela
33 empathy
34 gamboge
35 glockenspiel
36 histrionic
37 jeremiad
38 malevolence
39 peroration
40 viaticum

Level 5
41 bridewell
42 contango
43 helve
44 inductance
45 kelp
46 lune
47 mephitic
48 perique
49 semantic
50 thalamus

Level 6
51 chela
52 demurrage
53 fenestella
54 glyph
55 illation
56 limaceous
57 panurgic
58 rabbet
59 scrimshaw
60 sudd

Test No. 17

Level 1
1. anemone
2. balance
3. catalogue
4. decoration
5. horrid
6. insect
7. language
8. modern
9. obedient
10. pilgrim

Level 2
11. application
12. benefit
13. crater
14. demonstration
15. factor
16. hitch
17. jury
18. loiter
19. mildew
20. ordeal

Level 3
21. abdicate
22. catastrophe
23. impresario
24. irreparable
25. linear
26. mercantile
27. nitrogen
28. officious
29. perspective
30. radiant

Level 4
31. almoner
32. bibliography
33. cognate
34. daguerreotype
35. homonym
36. largesse
37. malign
38. minuend
39. neap
40. penultimate

Level 5
41. avatar
42. cheval-glass
43. demiurge
44. farandole
45. homocentric
46. kaolin
47. leat
48. llancro
49. marram
50. onager

Level 6
51. ablation
52. chalk-stone
53. gorcock
54. lampion
55. moxa
56. pyrene
57. scrannel
58. stirps
59. xenolith
60. yapp

Test No. 18

Level 1

 1 ascend
 2 balcony
 3 conclusion
 4 hobby
 5 marsh
 6 obstacle
 7 overtake
 8 pedestrian
 9 remainder
10 tow

Level 2

11 apparatus
12 clearance
13 derailment
14 hoard
15 ideal
16 joggle
17 malaria
18 meteor
19 obstinate
20 pedigree

Level 3

21 biennial
22 clarify
23 decathlon
24 figment
25 haggard
26 inundate
27 landward
28 minuet
29 nebula
30 radical

Level 4

31 amoral
32 basset
33 coterie
34 efferent
35 heterogeneous
36 inquisitorial
37 junta
38 libation
39 metamorphosis
40 rapine

Level 5

41 andiron
42 catharsis
43 digraph
44 eclogue
45 hippocampus
46 isogon
47 radicle
48 reagent
49 sackbut
50 valency

Level 6

51 chalcedony
52 feoffee
53 gombroon
54 laevulose
55 marasmus
56 mungo
57 quidnunc
58 tinnitus
59 ullage
60 velar

Test No. 19

Level 1

 1 almond
 2 buoy
 3 cul-de-sac
 4 gosling
 5 haste
 6 impersonate
 7 polite
 8 punctual
 9 source
10 traitor

Level 2

11 artificial
12 blunder
13 contrary
14 lurch
15 medieval
16 muzzle
17 perpendicular
18 predominate
19 submerge
20 turmoil

Level 3

21 anonymous
22 boycott
23 caustic
24 crescendo
25 depleted
26 essence
27 gist
28 hysterical
29 insipid
30 saturate

Level 4

31 casement
32 decrement
33 capalier
34 lampoon
35 minutiae
36 ocular
37 canivorous
38 raucous
39 replicate
40 sedulous

Level 5

41 arcanum
42 chervil
43 intaglio
44 mitraillouse
45 ossicle
46 pachydermatous
47 pleonasm
48 scree
49 symbiosis
50 veridical

Level 6

51 anchylosis
52 crambo
53 killick
54 mumpsimus
55 ogdoad
56 orthodromy
57 paduasey
58 runcinate
59 sphagnum
60 syrinx

Test No. 20

Level 1	Level 2	Level 3
1 belfry	11 besiege	21 aquiline
2 bulge	12 bronze	22 botanist
3 outlaw	13 gorge	23 captious
4 package	14 import	24 furtive
5 pillar	15 judo	25 initiate
6 rental	16 ledger	26 jaded
7 riddle	17 limpet	27 kaleidoscopic
8 shell-fish	18 penetrate	28 limerick
9 vanish	19 resort	29 mutual
10 varnish	20 warbler	30 stratagem

Level 4	Level 5	Level 6
31 aurochs	41 bergamot	51 ablegate
32 beriberi	42 brevier	52 algorism
33 cornice	43 deemster	53 baltimore
34 denary	44 homologous	54 bezel
35 gratuitous	45 lamina	55 leat
36 hertz	46 largo	56 mittimus
37 hiatus	47 pantheon	57 myosote
38 medial	48 refulgence	58 peneplain
39 teredo	49 savory	59 prunella
40 valetudinarian	50 triolet	60 windlestraw

Test No. 21

Level 1
1 altitude
2 bamboo
3 carpenter
4 express
5 lantern
6 massacre
7 octopus
8 partner
9 stomach
10 temperature

Level 2
11 aeronaut
12 detail
13 geographical
14 intercept
15 locality
16 patchwork
17 swerve
18 tidal
19 turbulent
20 wedge

Level 3
21 altimeter
22 caption
23 debris
24 hovel
25 insidious
26 libellous
27 obelisk
28 pastel
29 random
30 stolid

Level 4
31 aconite
32 calumny
33 decalogue
34 egocentric
35 gelid
36 ideograph
37 laudatory
38 massif
39 node
40 odium

Level 5
41 barbel
42 coenobite
43 demijohn
44 geodesy
45 helianthus
46 lacuna
47 maunder
48 noetic
49 octroi
50 squill

Level 6
51 bascule
52 cangue
53 gavelkind
54 hickwall
55 laparotomy
56 oliver
57 pasquinade
58 quiddity
59 salangane
60 tectonics

Test No. 22

Level 1
1 appointment
2 basin
3 calendar
4 cartridge
5 decrease
6 fossil
7 horrible
8 initials
9 lukewarm
10 margin

Level 2
11 bollard
12 depot
13 identity
14 luxury
15 masterly
16 miscalculate
17 occasional
18 peevish
19 sidle
20 tether

Level 3
21 abstemious
22 biology
23 cascade
24 derelict
25 felon
26 implacable
27 intervene
28 land-locked
29 lustre
30 menial

Level 4
31 asperity
32 Bushido
33 chimera
34 glossary
35 incarcerate
36 juxtapose
37 mendicant
38 nebulous
39 polyglot
40 referendum

Level 5
41 amice
42 caryatide
43 extragalactic
44 ghyll
45 lagan
46 manioc
47 parvis
48 sebaceous
49 sphygmograph
50 tarragon

Level 6
51 aegrotat
52 butterbump
53 clairschach
54 dalmatic
55 harmala
56 leister
57 machicolation
58 rhotacism
59 saccadic
60 teratology

Test No. 23

Level 1
1. arrival
2. bracken
3. corridor
4. kilt
5. opportunity
6. pastime
7. punishment
8. resemble
9. sparkle
10. windbreak

Level 2
11. beaker
12. impertinent
13. lather
14. medieval
15. piston
16. quadruped
17. requisite
18. tortuous
19. vault
20. wallet

Level 3
21. crucible
22. detonate
23. exonerate
24. fulcrum
25. hustle
26. instigate
27. Jacobite
28. limpid
29. symmetrical
30. tactile

Level 4
31. arbalest
32. collateral
33. doctrinaire
34. expiate
35. fugue
36. latchet
37. mordant
38. narcissism
39. planchette
40. sporadic

Level 5
41. binomial
42. bombasine
43. glossal
44. hornblende
45. lapsus calami
46. maya
47. orgulu
48. paediatrics
49. porphyry
50. wilding

Level 6
51. axolotl
52. blunge
53. chirograph
54. cromlech
55. hypocycloid
56. ontogenesis
57. oubliette
58. runt
59. sorghum
60. variorum

Test No. 24

Level 1
1 asphalt
2 carol
3 desert
4 encyclopedia
5 oblong
6 paragraph
7 rafter
8 scale
9 scarcity
10 trapeze

Level 2
11 asterisk
12 centigrade
13 density
14 estuary
15 negative
16 perforated
17 radius
18 section
19 solitary
20 superfluous

Level 3
21 absorbent
22 carnage
23 deluge
24 eliminate
25 negotiate
26 parole
27 recalcitrant
28 rudimentary
29 stringent
30 translucent

Level 4
31 acrimony
32 bauxite
33 cachet
34 denouement
35 egregious
36 obeisance
37 paradox
38 rationale
39 sacrosanct
40 zany

Level 5
41 anabaptist
42 chiaroscuro
43 dragoman
44 eidolon
45 nenuphar
46 parallax
47 parang
48 recalescence
49 rococo
50 subpoena

Level 6
51 alburnum
52 cacique
53 dunnage
54 enclitic
55 niello
56 paraheliotropism
57 radula
58 rocambole
59 surrebutter
60 talus

Test No. 25

Level 1	Level 2	Level 3
1 anthill	11 absurd	21 acoustics
2 climate	12 collapse	22 bicker
3 container	13 entire	23 bison
4 endeavour	14 generation	24 centripetal
5 immediately	15 immigrate	25 emancipation
6 jingle	16 jealous	26 garbled
7 outcast	17 mature	27 lichen
8 rhyme	18 raid	28 mattock
9 signal	19 satellite	29 outshine
10 tank	20 slipshod	30 perimeter

Level 4	Level 5	Level 6
31 botulism	41 chamfer	51 champlève
32 cataneous	42 eschatology	52 deadlight
33 datum	43 giaour	53 enchiridion
34 *distrait*	44 imprest	54 goetic
35 encyclical	45 lapidate	55 jokul
36 gamma	46 nadir	56 laches
37 lacerate	47 oblate	57 maud
38 mandate	48 samphire	58 pedicular
39 martinet	49 satrap	59 spandrel
40 nacelle	50 ukase	60 vavasour

Test No. 26

Level 1
1 boomerang
2 invention
3 invitation
4 planet
5 puncture
6 quantity
7 recipe
8 time-table
9 torrential
10 vehicle

Level 2
11 aviation
12 curb
13 guillotine
14 haphazard
15 indefinite
16 ludicrous
17 monsoon
18 perpetual
19 regional
20 tributary

Level 3
21 antipodes
22 bulwark
23 commonplace
24 deterrent
25 irrational
26 legislate
27 lenient
28 minion
29 obstreperous
30 tabulate

Level 4
31 aneroid
32 breve
33 carboy
34 criterion
35 dormer
36 terminology
37 tautology
38 unguent
39 variance
40 whitesmith

Level 5
41 brevet
42 gibbous
43 humoresque
44 jongleur
45 lateen
46 lazaretto
47 palmyra
48 penetralia
49 recidivism
50 trounce

Level 6
51 adiaphorism
52 gadroon
53 hyson
54 jacquerie
55 lexigraphy
56 peristalith
57 quoin
58 reify
59 virgule
60 wayzgoose

Test No. 27

Level 1	Level 2	Level 3
1 barge	11 astronomer	21 abscond
2 cable	12 banish	22 barrage
3 continent	13 camouflage	23 calibre
4 exactly	14 excess	24 elliptical
5 habit	15 fallow	25 financial
6 landlord	16 obliterate	26 negligent
7 mascot	17 optimism	27 nocturnal
8 orchestra	18 twinge	28 ritual
9 passport	19 tyranny	29 stoic
10 resolve	20 unassuming	30 typical

Level 4	Level 5	Level 6
31 anachronism	41 azoic	51 anacoluthon
32 analgesic	42 behemoth	52 banket
33 bathos	43 calx	53 cadastre
34 cacophony	44 foudroyant	54 dalton
35 diatom	45 rondeau	55 fumatory
36 empirical	46 sansculotte	56 netsuke
37 Nemesis	47 sillabub	57 pandect
38 rondo	48 tympanum	58 runagate
39 ubiquity	49 uhlan	59 systaltic
40 vignette	50 xenophobia	60 thurifer

Test No. 28

Level 1
 1 basket-ball
 2 courage
 3 gleam
 4 ivory
 5 launch
 6 leash
 7 monarchy
 8 protect
 9 valley
10 watertight

Level 2
11 agile
12 bragging
13 cape
14 host
15 mutiny
16 proclamation
17 propaganda
18 universal
19 vagabond
20 water-logged

Level 3
21 bolster
22 combustion
23 diaphragm
24 extraneous
25 filament
26 humus
27 hypoteneuse
28 interloper
29 opaque
30 parsimony

Level 4
31 counterpoint
32 endemic
33 foment
34 lamprey
35 myopic
36 nascent
37 nuance
38 paean
39 parabola
40 repository

Level 5
41 attainder
42 bouleversement
43 coloratura
44 hygrometer
45 lien
46 moa
47 palanquin
48 solenoid
49 suture
50 transom

Level 6
51 almagest
52 burin
53 nonce
54 oenometer
55 orectic
56 repoussage
57 tanistry
58 umbo
59 virelay
60 windrow

Test No. 29

Level 1

1 automatic
2 cluster
3 comedy
4 imagine
5 maze
6 padlock
7 separate
8 similar
9 thermometer
10 tighten

Level 2

11 arena
12 cavity
13 constellation
14 contraband
15 monotonous
16 reckless
17 reservoir
18 scaffolding
19 tornado
20 vowel

Level 3

21 augment
22 convex
23 enigmatic
24 habitable
25 jettison
26 literal
27 ornithology
28 pageant
29 truculent
30 wizened

Level 4

31 aura
32 brio
33 caprice
34 cryptography
35 diphthong
36 distraint
37 friable
38 litany
39 modus
40 retina

Level 5

41 adumbrate
42 carapace
43 crapulous
44 curmudgeon
45 distich
46 forensic
47 persona
48 plangent
49 sortilege
50 spatchcock

Level 6

51 anadromous
52 aphesis
53 barratry
54 lauwine
55 miniver
56 mundungus
57 scaramouch
58 timothy
59 windage
60 yogh

Test No. 30

Level 1
1. humbug
2. ivy
3. legend
4. magnet
5. nickname
6. probably
7. ripple
8. situation
9. tattoo
10. theatre

Level 2
11. autobiography
12. corrugated
13. extinct
14. gladiator
15. deputy
16. hooligan
17. lanky
18. magistrate
19. nozzle
20. offend

Level 3
21. alloy
22. brevity
23. deportation
24. hinterland
25. inscrutable
26. lineage
27. mucilage
28. omen
29. persecute
30. repertoire

Level 4
31. agoraphobia
32. barograph
33. concatenation
34. demography
35. hierarchy
36. ice-blink
37. megrim
38. olfactory
39. radian
40. risotto

Level 5
41. animism
42. boulevardier
43. canticle
44. homophone
45. lammergeyer
46. mangonel
47. natterjack
48. palaeozoic
49. peignoir
50. reticle

Level 6
51. acarpous
52. chanterelle
53. demersal
54. eclampsia
55. gonfalon
56. jeofail
57. orris
58. pyx
59. ret
60. sachem

Test No. 31

Level 1
1 pantomime
2 numeral
3 recent
4 restaurant
5 sail
6 skilful
7 temperate
8 ventriloquist
9 wreck
10 yacht

Level 2
11 heave
12 meditate
13 pedestal
14 preoccupation
15 rally
16 ramble
17 roost
18 strenuous
19 walrus
20 zinc

Level 3
21 illogical
22 mastery
23 notorious
24 obsolescent
25 ohm
26 pathetic
27 raillery
28 sacrifice
29 unanimous
30 zoologist

Level 4
31 hauteur
32 id
33 mayhem
34 nimbus
35 occlusion
36 patrician
37 sybaritic
38 trapezium
39 vortex
40 wampum

Level 5
41 grilse
42 hirsute
43 imprimatur
44 jolly-boat
45 kukri
46 ogive
47 onomatopoeia
48 parhelion
49 rugose
50 tarantella

Level 6
51 haustellum
52 meninx
53 noctule
54 omphalus
55 reticulum
56 rouleau
57 tabes
58 thalamite
59 vehmgericht
60 zygmurgy

Test No. 32

Level 1
1 accident
2 baton
3 dairy
4 expect
5 frequent
6 notch
7 occupant
8 ocean
9 porpoise
10 prairie

Level 2
11 ability
12 battalion
13 caper
14 enamel
15 flabby
16 girder
17 glacier
18 morsel
19 observatory
20 portable

Level 3
21 abacus
22 canopy
23 dais
24 emigrate
25 excise
26 fabric
27 mortar
28 nucleus
29 pompous
30 portray

Level 4
31 abrasive
32 canton
33 descant
34 devolution
35 etymology
36 extradition
37 fricassee
38 ichneumon
39 portage
40 quintessence

Level 5
41 abiogenesis
42 canzonet
43 dacoit
44 ergotism
45 fissile
46 föhn
47 nugatory
48 pragmatic
49 quartile
50 quittance

Level 6
51 abomasum
52 batfowling
53 canterbury
54 detent
55 encaustic
56 fisc
57 frisket
58 girandole
59 idioticon
60 mordent

Test No. 33

Level 1
1 comma
2 dew
3 future
4 improvement
5 loft
6 machinery
7 population
8 rifle
9 tremble
10 voyage

Level 2
11 criminal
12 hurdle
13 implement
14 indebted
15 luxuriant
16 mercury
17 prosperous
18 reject
19 vacuum
20 volume

Level 3
21 devoid
22 hypnotic
23 irrevocable
24 laminated
25 malnutrition
26 obnoxious
27 persuasive
28 trilogy
29 vassal
30 witticism

Level 4
31 didactic
32 dissemble
33 germane
34 hypercritical
35 imponderable
36 kilter
37 Lamarckian
38 restitution
39 transcendental
40 vestigial

Level 5
41 cryptogam
42 deponent
43 fluxion
44 ganglion
45 heuristic
46 kedge
47 logomachy
48 martlet
49 Ostpolitik
50 wyvern

Level 6
51 gibus
52 gyromancy
53 hypallage
54 kanaka
55 lipper
56 lycanthropy
57 mandrel
58 megasse
59 parpen
60 serac

Test No. 34

Level 1
1 badge
2 carve
3 dawn
4 fist
5 gang
6 hovercraft
7 idle
8 junior
9 seldom
10 thaw

Level 2
11 barrier
12 ceremony
13 genius
14 haunted
15 inspect
16 method
17 narrative
18 shear
19 squad
20 threshold

Level 3
21 abashed
22 ballast
23 candid
24 concentric
25 genealogy
26 impromptu
27 itinerant
28 liberal
29 modify
30 papyrus

Level 4
31 beck
32 cirrus
33 gamut
34 hidalgo
35 julep
36 littoral
37 malleable
38 nullify
39 selenium
40 tenuous

Level 5
41 aberglaube
42 carrel
43 gemmate
44 landau
45 listerine
46 Mohock
47 obsidian
48 paraclete
49 quintain
50 sophism

Level 6
51 aberdevine
52 garboard
53 hoplite
54 izard
55 launce
56 malism
57 rilletts
58 roquelaure
59 satyagraha
60 sejant

Test No. 35

Level 1	Level 2	Level 3
1 badger	11 brewer	21 breaker
2 capture	12 charity	22 cumbersome
3 fresh	13 generosity	23 detention
4 hiss	14 idol	24 fumigate
5 ironmonger	15 lathe	25 humane
6 ladle	16 orderly	26 juggernaut
7 mermaid	17 orient	27 kayak
8 parade	18 quest	28 lineal
9 rear	19 rowlock	29 objective
10 swindle	20 summit	30 sorcery

Level 4	Level 5	Level 6
31 chicanery	41 ablaut	51 chibouk
32 gravamen	42 belvedere	52 disembogue
33 holocaust	43 dimity	53 gemmule
34 lethargic	44 gelation	54 idolum
35 monograph	45 homoeopathy	55 lasque
36 pinnace	46 morpheme	56 oreide
37 ramify	47 *pis aller*	57 quintan
38 scrutineer	48 psephology	58 rampion
39 tangential	49 regulus	59 scammony
40 unction	50 sawder	60 sullage

Test No. 36

Level 1	Level 2	Level 3
1 accept	11 bondage	21 cyclonic
2 dictation	12 casualty	22 duress
3 fortune	13 diameter	23 fervid
4 humorous	14 eruption	24 grandiose
5 interest	15 hindrance	25 immoderate
6 manger	16 knead	26 obtrude
7 orchard	17 lop-sided	27 rarefied
8 punch	18 navigation	28 satiate
9 reptile	19 oral	29 subjugate
10 scorching	20 panorama	30 unison

Level 4	Level 5	Level 6
31 achromatic	41 basil	51 acrophobia
32 beleaguer	42 catalepsy	52 barbara
33 calibrate	43 eyas	53 cay
34 consortium	44 fumitory	54 estreat
35 euphoria	45 geotropism	55 fraise
36 *feuilleton*	46 kissing-crust	56 opsonic
37 hormone	47 levanter	57 panopticon
38 irrefragable	48 messuage	58 piaffe
39 juncture	49 pleasance	59 saffian
40 pundit	50 quadriga	60 sprue

Test No. 37

Level 1
1 annoying
2 border
3 calm
4 deck
5 fence
6 gripping
7 hook
8 lodging
9 oval
10 scrape

Level 2
11 antler
12 certificate
13 deserted
14 fluid
15 frank
16 livelihood
17 native
18 parish
19 range
20 shaggy

Level 3
21 avaricious
22 convection
23 detain
24 entomology
25 hypocrite
26 imprudent
27 leverage
28 liniment
29 pseudonym
30 segregate

Level 4
31 antibody
32 cuneiform
33 ductile
34 fortuitous
35 gneiss
36 impugn
37 ling
38 sardonic
39 talisman
40 vestigial

Level 5
41 apogee
42 calefactory
43 diamagnetic
44 enfilade
45 hebetude
46 Jeroboam
47 lexical
48 lunette
49 octant
50 parieal

Level 6
51 bullace
52 chert
53 francolin
54 heddles
55 jarl
56 kaross
57 lambrequin
58 morion
59 pandect
60 quenelle

Test No. 38

Level 1
1. audience
2. ceiling
3. crumble
4. edge
5. harbour
6. leopard
7. outer
8. protect
9. rook
10. shrink

Level 2
11. axis
12. backing
13. embroidery
14. fingerprint
15. glossy
16. harrow
17. interference
18. liberty
19. matchless
20. serialize

Level 3
21. creditable
22. despotic
23. furore
24. gullible
25. ostentatious
26. potential
27. receptive
28. rotate
29. sessional
30. stalemate

Level 4
31. anthropomorphic
32. cortical
33. fractious
34. horologist
35. immure
36. misogynist
37. occultism
38. pervasive
39. touchstone
40. virulent

Level 5
41. anopheles
42. burnet
43. cusec
44. embolism
45. grackle
46. illuminati
47. orlop
48. putative
49. scabrous
50. swinge

Level 6
51. anoetic
52. banneret
53. distichous
54. egger
55. enzootic
56. fenks
57. ginglymus
58. incivism
59. loricate
60. megilp

Test No. 39

<table>
<tr><td>

Level 1

1 advertisement
2 broadcast
3 chapter
4 drama
5 faulty
6 glide
7 island
8 jet
9 lake
10 mule

</td><td>

Level 2

11 ambitious
12 draughty
13 famine
14 grouse
15 joint
16 latch
17 noteworthy
18 offering
19 parable
20 radar

</td><td>

Level 3

21 amenable
22 brogue
23 concussion
24 epigram
25 facsimile
26 gizzard
27 inedible
28 involuntary
29 legacy
30 myriad

</td></tr>
<tr><td>

Level 4

31 arpeggio
32 bevel
33 diurnal
34 franchise
35 immunology
36 nefarious
37 obscurantism
38 theodolite
39 torsion
40 verve

</td><td>

Level 5

41 capote
42 dentine
43 diarchy
44 espièglerie
45 exegetical
46 faucal
47 gingko
48 inlier
49 lipography
50 pantagruelian

</td><td>

Level 6

51 amygdalic
52 clypeus
53 dedans
54 firman
55 gunter
56 istle
57 lias
58 mistigris
59 nuncupate
60 tortious

</td></tr>
</table>

Test No. 40

Level 1
1. batter
2. chest
3. engineer
4. funnel
5. horn
6. mean
7. outrun
8. pickaxe
9. remove
10. search

Level 2
11. barbed
12. chemistry
13. exception
14. fascinating
15. gibberish
16. hydrogen
17. Latin
18. microscope
19. shield
20. suburb

Level 3
21. dabble
22. exhaustive
23. filtrate
24. garnish
25. indifferent
26. kaiser
27. metronome
28. naïve
29. patronize
30. reinforce

Level 4
31. betise
32. clamant
33. dirigible
34. epitome
35. histrionic
36. logarithm
37. panegyric
38. rowel
39. simoom
40. stricture

Level 5
41. apercu
42. bleb
43. decorticate
44. gauss
45. involute
46. lambent
47. peculation
48. recidivist
49. semiotics
50. speculum

Level 6
51. crucian
52. deuteragonist
53. encaustic
54. hoveller
55. immortelle
56. limpkin
57. mort
58. peen
59. regelate
60. sandiver

Test No. 41

Level 1
 1 arrest
 2 blaze
 3 couple
 4 factory
 5 grain
 6 narrow
 7 queue
 8 relative
 9 scribble
10 type

Level 2
11 anticipate
12 arctic
13 canvas
14 detour
15 enterprising
16 fertile
17 hamper
18 infrequent
19 liquidize
20 stern

Level 3
21 brawny
22 condensed
23 ebb
24 gimlet
25 harangue
26 impregnable
27 lax
28 maritime
29 negligible
30 sanguinary

Level 4
31 advocacy
32 benign
33 comfit
34 harbinger
35 interstice
36 *mélange*
37 necromancy
38 plasma
39 retroactive
40 scrutator

Level 5
41 escheat
42 insolation
43 knag
44 monstrance
45 obsecration
46 prothalamium
47 recusant
48 secant
49 troika
50 vulpine

Level 6
51 brassage
52 condyle
53 dammar
54 gobemouche
55 logie
56 Nearctic
57 obeah
58 sanicle
59 trommel
60 whangee

Test No. 42

Level 1	Level 2	Level 3
1 bruise	11 browse	21 brusque
2 cobweb	12 energetic	22 coax
3 dismiss	13 fen	23 distraction
4 endless	14 husky	24 girth
5 fashion	15 jig	25 jargon
6 hymn	16 memory	26 manqué
7 magpie	17 neglect	27 narcissus
8 nibble	18 obtain	28 obviate
9 office	19 peasant	29 paltry
10 pebble	20 polar	30 quarantine

Level 4	Level 5	Level 6
31 bryony	41 appellate	51 buccinator
32 cochlea	42 *bonne bouche*	52 coalmouse
33 dosage	43 capacitor	53 dittography
34 emollient	44 echinoderm	54 fartlek
35 extrapolate	45 glaive	55 glair
36 gudgeon	46 guichet	56 haras
37 hyperbolic	47 jeremiad	57 nattier blue
38 quantify	48 loosestrife	58 panada
39 retribution	49 podium	59 razee
40 teasel	50 triptych	60 sastrugi

Test No. 43

Level 1
1 brooch
2 gallop
3 kennel
4 mention
5 pare
6 pier
7 recognize
8 salad
9 selfish
10 tender

Level 2
11 ambush
12 bleach
13 decrease
14 elastic
15 elaction
16 fatal
17 imitate
18 lukewarm
19 vowel
20 telescopic

Level 3
21 amenity
22 blatant
23 collaborator
24 decoy
25 façade
26 goad
27 herbal
28 immobilize
29 sedge
30 technology

Level 4
31 *amende honorable*
32 brigantine
33 cantilever
34 embrasure
35 fardel
36 genetics
37 ibis
38 knout
39 module
40 nominative

Level 5
41 bergschrund
42 gnosis
43 hepatic
44 lenity
45 lucubration
46 machete
47 noisette
48 pavan
49 quartan
50 rinderpest

Level 6
51 bombardon
52 cancellated
53 cold short
54 deeping
55 elecampane
56 flustra
57 hippocras
58 kerf
59 pandour
60 tellurian

Test No. 44

Level 1
1 backbone
2 chop
3 echo
4 elm
5 harm
6 poultry
7 powder
8 rudder
9 ruin
10 swarm

Level 2
11 abbot
12 bachelor
13 cobbled
14 domestic
15 frail
16 grating
17 harsh
18 quiver
19 scornful
20 squander

Level 3
21 bedraggled
22 distributor
23 executor
24 furrowed
25 maternal
26 palate
27 premier
28 residue
29 straggling
30 tumultuous

Level 4
31 Aaron's rod
32 barcarole
33 basalt
34 candescent
35 emanation
36 fiduciary
37 glottal
38 *hortus siccus*
39 prevaricate
40 rapacious

Level 5
41 abatis
42 *démenti*
43 feverfew
44 *hachure*
45 latifundia
46 persimmon
47 quaternion
48 rhumb
49 shagreen
50 thaumaturgy

Level 6
51 aam
52 barbule
53 drail
54 graticulation
55 halitus
56 jugulate
57 lordosis
58 morbidezza
59 palstave
60 quebracho

Test No. 45

Level 1
1 battery
2 carnation
3 drowsy
4 forecast
5 guilty
6 jelly-fish
7 mention
8 pathless
9 result
10 screen

Level 2
11 crag
12 dwindling
13 easterly
14 hilt
15 impetuous
16 instinct
17 pike
18 regulation
19 verge
20 warehouse

Level 3
21 bristling
22 devious
23 entangle
24 mere
25 precipitous
26 scurvy
27 summons
28 territorial
29 unkempt
30 vindicate

Level 4
31 burnous
32 cadenza
33 debenture
34 flench
35 franklin
36 habergeon
37 *ignis fatuus*
38 jocund
39 mutability
40 napoleon

Level 5
41 catchpole
42 Greek Calends
43 Heaviside Layer
44 ichor
45 jussive
46 limen
47 nescience
48 obi
49 panhandle
50 ramose

Level 6
51 calamary
52 eparch
53 fleury
54 grangerise
55 jacobus
56 levigate
57 marshalsea
58 narthex
59 obol
60 tetterwort

Test No. 46

Level 1
1 aim
2 century
3 hoarse
4 iceberg
5 keen
6 numb
7 obstacle
8 pistol
9 raft
10 rink

Level 2
11 acid
12 device
13 halo
14 kink
15 least
16 oddity
17 plaster
18 rack
19 scour
20 tempest

Level 3
21 aileron
22 brackish
23 cantankerous
24 dowser
25 gratify
26 heckle
27 immersion
28 kestrel
29 leaven
30 sump

Level 4
31 adipose
32 cerements
33 granitic
34 hedonism
35 immutable
36 kinetic
37 leach
38 mastic
39 nubile
40 oesophagus

Level 5
41 *à huis clos*
42 greave
43 holt
44 imagist
45 Manichee
46 ogee
47 pismire
48 saltire
49 telergy
50 usufruct

Level 6
51 ahimsa
52 cere
53 entasis
54 gralloch
55 hoggin
56 impanate
57 kalong
58 mastaba
59 Notogaea
60 pintle

Test No. 47

Level 1	Level 2	Level 3
1 bitter	11 buoyant	21 burnished
2 compass	12 compress	22 deflate
3 dial	13 defy	23 dismantle
4 ferret	14 ferocious	24 engrave
5 helm	15 fraud	25 flaccid
6 illustrated	16 grill	26 gratuity
7 jumble	17 hardy	27 *hors de combat*
8 lair	18 illusion	28 impinge
9 noose	19 leisure	29 isotherm
10 scar	20 semi-colon	30 justiciary

Level 4	Level 5	Level 6
31 bibulous	41 bunt	51 bergmehl
32 colloquy	42 diablerie	52 colophony
33 defalcation	43 engross	53 dogger
34 enjambment	44 *en prise*	54 frazie
35 hegira	45 Fraunhofer lines	55 greenlet
36 huckster	46 gnostic	56 haplography
37 labial	47 headstall	57 izzard
38 latitudinarian	48 lavabo	58 menhir
39 marjoram	49 macramé	59 opsimathy
40 obsequies	50 ogham	60 piddock

Test No. 48

Level 1
1 avoid
2 interior
3 jerk
4 keyboard
5 nuisance
6 overturn
7 quart
8 register
9 skull
10 washer

Level 2
11 instantly
12 loophole
13 numerous
14 overland
15 pursuit
16 rejoice
17 solar
18 tentacle
19 urgent
20 waltz

Level 3
21 mural
22 niggling
23 purloin
24 quartz
25 rodent
26 soliloquize
27 tendril
28 usury
29 vulnerable
30 waspish

Level 4
31 limber
32 nova
33 ouzel
34 point-device
35 quatrain
36 rhetorical
37 somatic
38 termagant
39 uvula
40 volute

Level 5
41 fovea
42 hodiernal
43 interlard
44 jointure
45 lorcha
46 murex
47 nonage
48 purslane
49 quadrature
50 vinculum

Level 6
51 brocket
52 jumbal
53 kermes
54 nutation
55 puteal
56 revet
57 somite
58 tenson
59 vomer
60 zymotic

Test No. 49

Level 1
1. amazed
2. belfry
3. cautious
4. distant
5. explain
6. guide
7. modern
8. season
9. soot
10. tame

Level 2
11. acute
12. callous
13. diplomatic
14. entrant
15. feint
16. gender
17. hawk-eyed
18. minimum
19. professional
20. quartet

Level 3
21. alleviate
22. category
23. dissuade
24. ego
25. indecision
26. levy
27. millennium
28. pedantic
29. tariff
30. vestige

Level 4
31. contingency
32. emolument
33. felicitous
34. malaise
35. meticulous
36. proctor
37. revert
38. trauma
39. vicissitude
40. volition

Level 5
41. apothegm
42. cathode
43. courgette
44. draconian
45. exegesis
46. *glissando*
47. pomander
48. scrip
49. tong
50. vesicular

Level 6
51. brandreth
52. corposant
53. euphorbia
54. glendoveer
55. mandamus
56. myoclonic
57. reseda
58. saxatile
59. smallage
60. trave

Test No. 50

Level 1

1 annual
2 buffalo
3 clatter
4 daring
5 fold
6 gaping
7 harpoon
8 lend
9 mineral
10 pliers

Level 2

11 charter
12 dappled
13 disown
14 flurried
15 half-hearted
16 hardware
17 lens
18 Morse code
19 observation
20 physical

Level 3

21 assiduous
22 autonomy
23 bureaucracy
24 clairvoyant
25 deference
26 idiom
27 renegade
28 tenacious
29 tribunal
30 verdigris

Level 4

31 accoutrement
32 contrition
33 convertibility
34 dissimulate
35 exemplar
36 garrulity
37 ingratiate
38 parochialism
39 penalogical
40 vagary

Level 5

41 annuitant
42 cabriole
43 daedal
44 Diktat
45 *éminence grise*
46 esurient
47 marline
48 lei
49 plethoric
50 numinous

Level 6

51 bulimia
52 chert
53 estovers
54 frisket
55 jynx
56 mora
57 placer
58 putlog
59 *ranz des vaches*
60 setwall